BALANCE

BALANCE

Living a Life True to Yourself

Marina Fernández Julián

A CIP catalogue record for this title is available from the British Library.

ISBN: (Paperback edition) 978-1-7398638-0-7
ISBN: (Digital edition) 978-1-7398638-1-4

Get the FREE Guide *The 11 Pillars of Inner Balance* at
https://www.marinazestforlife.com/balance-giveaway

Edited and produced by Deborah Taylor: booklaunchyourbusiness.com

Page design and layout by Catherine Williams: chapter-one-book-production.co.uk

Cover design by Andy Prior: andypriordesign.co.uk

Illustrations by Lisa Ashton: coneyhurststudios.co.uk

Author photography by Giles Hampton: 500px.com/gileshampton

Disclaimer
This is a work of non-fiction. Nonetheless, the names, personal characteristics of individuals, and details of events have been changed in order to disguise identities or protect the privacy of the author's clients and students. Any resulting resemblance to persons living or dead is entirely coincidental and unintentional. The author of this book does not dispense medical advice or prescribe the use of any technique, euther directly or indirectly, as a form of treatment for physical, emotional, or medical problems, without the advice of a physician. The author's intent is only to offer information of a general nature to help you in you quest for emotional, physical, and spiritual well-being. In the event you use any of the information in this book, the author and the publisher assume no responsibility for your actions.

Dedication

To you Elo,
Your eyes told me a story:
If we don't live, love and act now … When?
Thank you for inspiring me to walk the talk,
for the laughter and the tears.

Reviews

Here is a small sample of some of the reviews of *Balance*.

> *"Marina's book is a beautiful as she is. It has been my honour to accompany Marina as part of her learning journey and to witness the treasure that she has produced here. Just the process of reading this book will undoubtedly light up your life and bring you the balance you seek. Marina's rich words and the situations she describes are powerful and heart touching because this is an expression of Marina herself and the way she lives her life. Marina most definitely walks her talk. Thank you, Marina. It is a delight."*
>
> Sue Knight, Master Trainer of NLP
> and author of *NLP at Work*

> *"Marina's book is as warm, fun-filled and practical as the virtual kitchen in which it is set. It reads like a conversation with Marina: compassionate, inspiring and full of zest. I love the activities in each chapter which invite the reader to move from simply considering the ideas, to engaging with them*

and applying them practically. It eschews perfectionism, accepts the frailties of human beings and celebrates our ability to make real change so we can live life to the full. I'm inspired!"

Florence Madden, Accredited NLP Trainer,
author of *The Intention Impact Conundrum*
and co-author of *Everyday NLP*

"Highly recommended!!! Marina's book is very empowering, motivating and inspiring. It's the kind of book that aligns your consciousness with your will, so that you can live more freely and consciously in accordance with who you are and whatever your calling is. The book can be read from beginning to end or simply by choosing whichever chapter speaks to you at the tine. I loved this book – it activated my inner awareness and stimulated my desire to keep learning and growing. A great timeless reference."

Karen Koramshai, Model, foodie and wellness advocate
www.karenkoramshai.com

"This book is for everybody and at any stage in their lives. It truly gives the reader tools to help them become "the best version of themselves". The simplicity yet genius repeat at the end of each chapter in the 'Empowering Actions' and 'Zesty Takeaways' ensuring the reader deeply reflects and understands the changes needed to live their best life .

There are so many beautiful explanations in this book, and one in particular that had an impact is Marina's beautiful interpretation of the soul – it most certainly moved mine!

The soul gives us an awareness of our internal and external existence and this is the essence of our being."

Paula Seabourne, Founder of Minds Matter Now

"Do you sometimes wonder if you are living life or are you getting carried along with it? This book can help you get back in control and achieve a more fulfilled and happier life.

Marina takes you on a journey and gets you to focus on what is right and what is out of balance, and shares intimate experiences to help bring to life the questions you need to ask yourself. The book is packed with tips and simple exercises which can help you along your journey and you can go at your own pace. A light and powerful read."

Francesca Hampton,
Chief Financial Officer, Cynergy Bank

"Marina has created a real gem. A powerful and also playful book that keeps you wanting to go back to it. It is easy to read, to the point and inspiring to fearlessly take control of your life and 'change' into the best version of yourself."

Renate van Nijen, artist and writer,
www.renatevannijenfineart.com

Contents

My gratitude

I could write an entire book listing everyone I'm grateful to for helping me get to this point! It has been challenging to include everyone who's supported, inspired and encouraged me along the way.

First of all, I want to thank my clients for being my best teachers. Without your stories and experiences, this book would not have been possible. Your stories are important. They all deserve to be shared with respect and love. I feel honoured to have taken part in your journey, forever grateful.

To my husband and children, thank you for allowing me the space to write this book and for putting up with the many overcooked meals that I produced while my head was somewhere else; including the day I almost burned the kitchen down.

My deepest gratitude goes to Francesca Hampton for her continued faith in me, as well as her love, time, support and help with getting my message out in the world. I could not have done it without you as a torchbearer – and I mean it. Watching your life attentively has helped me understand that superheroes do exist after all, just not the way we thought they did. You prove that they're more powerful than the made-up ones! Your business brain and my unicorn world make the best team. You are actually a unicorn dressed in a power suit.

Hannah Havas, thank you for encouraging me to believe I could write a book before it was even a dream. Thank you for urging me to do it and for not letting me give up.

Emma Rion, my writing coach, when the book was just a collection of ideas, your questions ignited my soul and helped me bring the words to life.

Julie Parkin, you are on my list of essentials. Thank you for encouraging me to be the person I am meant to be. Our connection was arranged well before we met each other.

My almost sister and soulmate Eva Calle, you give me butterflies and we are experts at celebrating life together. Thank you for endlessly believing in me and for your admiration, it is mutual. Te quiero hasta la luna y Volver.

Lola Navarro!!! The best sex coach and adviser I've ever met; every person should have a Lola in their lives.

Dr Eva Orozco, your loving words bring out the best in me, I'm so lucky to have you in my life.

Clare Connelly, thank you for lovingly criticising my introduction. It helped me to bring out what I had inside me.

Jane Jones, you are more special than you know. Thank you for your input and support.

Manuel Fernandez, you are the wisest person I have ever met, thank you for your time, love and attention.

To all my friends: Yolanda, Sharon, Sacha, Nicky, Mila and many others. It would take a whole chapter to name you all. Thank you for loving me without wanting to change me.

My inner child, my best friend, I simply could not live without your presence in my world.

My family in Spain; you are my powerhouse and the source of my joy. I want to give a special mention to my mum and my sister. Having powerful women like you around me made me feel strong and safe.

My dad who, when I was 16 years old and fat, made me believe I was the most beautiful girl in the world. You made me believe in me – and I still do. I could have not wished for a better legacy, thank you!!!

Professor Jørgen Bering Asmussen, your constructive insights and clever questions made me jump from the lazy chair into work mode.

Dr Martin Valls, your patience is infinite. We spent the whole weekend operating on this book. The patients you care for as a doctor are lucky.

Sue Knight, thank you for being the sculptor of the magnificent project that is me! Thank you for your ongoing teaching; you have helped to shape my life. Even when you are not teaching me, I hear you. You are a master of NLP.

Deborah Taylor, the editor of this book. Perhaps the most important time for a book is when it falls into the hands of others. Thank you for making my words into a book worth reading. Thank you for your editing skills, your expert eye and for giving my book the love it deserves.

Lisa Ashton, thank you for sharing your talent in the illustrations for this book.

Thank you to everyone who made me the person I am today, for touching my heart and for allowing me to enter yours. No doubt the world is a better place with us in it.

Preface

It was in her last waking hours before my dear friend passed away that I saw it in her eyes – we only have one shot at life; and now is the time to live it.

I had travelled to see my friend back home in Spain. She'd had a transplant a few months before but had taken a turn for the worse. When I saw her, she was at home, pretending everything was going to be okay again in a few months, but we both knew she was dying.

As usual, she asked me for a hug and kiss, but I'd just come from the airport. I was carrying two small children who were full of cold and I feared any germs would kill her. So, I said I couldn't, that it wasn't safe for her, and I'd rather not take the risk.

At that moment, her eyes told me: "If you don't kiss me now… when will you?"

I don't think I'll ever forget that look.

The next time I saw her, she was in hospital. The doctors were waiting for her heart to stop beating. It was my last chance to see her. I asked if I could touch her. They said yes, it didn't matter anymore.

I sat and talked to her, touched her and kissed her with all the love I had in me. It sounds crazy to say it, yet by touching her, the pain I'd carried since the last time I'd seen her was released. She died a few hours later.

During the long night after her death, I reflected on how, throughout her journey, all she had ever wanted was love and connection. It is all any of us ever want.

"Life is lived in the extra beats we hold as time unfolds."
Brendon Burchard

In a strange way, her death set me free and healed me in ways I never thought possible. It hit me like a thunderbolt and woke me up to the realisation that we all have everything we need; we have forgotten how to make the most of life. That living our life fully means embracing the highs as well as the lows and, above all, that in order to experience and sustain balance, we need to live a life true to who we are, connecting to ourselves first.

Through this experience, I became more aware than ever that life comes as a one-way ticket and what we're really here to do is live, connect, love and thrive. It is our responsibility to choose how to live and our life will directly reflect those choices.

Never miss the chance to have an adventure, a hug, a kiss or some fun.

When my friend died, I knew I had a responsibility to spread this message. As a changemaker and someone who loves life, it is my mission to support those who have lost their joy for life and help them reclaim it.

Now I have your attention our journey begins.

Introduction

Over the years, through meditation and learning, I have experienced what feels to me like heaven on earth many times. Each time, it has come to me as a sense of balance and completeness. Let me share one particular experience with you so you can explore it too.

It was the end of a very intense and deep, year-long group training. In our last session together, our teacher asked us to create a metaphor that described how we saw ourselves and our lives now that the course was over.

As I closed my eyes, I saw clearly a spring surrounded by green, lush countryside. The trickling water was crystal clear, crisp, and fresh. It flowed gently, yet it was playful, perfectly balanced. Uncontained, light, and formless, this water was transparent. It was true to itself and simply kept doing what it was meant to do: sharing its life-giving essence and travelling to reach the places it was needed before finally flowing into the sea. It felt like heaven on earth.

It is my wish that what I share in this book helps you to find the same easy flow and balance; your own vision of heaven on earth.

"Live as if you were to die tomorrow.
Learn as if you were to live forever."

Mahatma Gandhi

How the book is organised

This book is divided into two parts. The first part gives you the tools to discover your inner resources and destination. The second part of the book is all about how you can add more connection and fun to your life. Together, they will help you achieve balance, zest and inner freedom. The result of this self-exploration releases an excellent version of you, someone true to yourself – a you that thrives, fulfils your potential and creates a life full of possibilities.

This is not another book about how to be successful, instead, it's a guide to help you explore and discover who you are and what you truly want. I'll be sharing tools, stories and wisdom to help you find out who is in the driving seat of your life. And if it's not you – or not the best version of you – I'll show you how to steer yourself in a different direction. I'm here to empower you to reach your potential and thrive, so you can live a great life.

Who is this book for?

This book is for you if:

- ✓ You're ready to make the most of your life and believe it has more to offer you.
- ✓ You want to achieve your goals and dreams without having to be someone you're not or needing to trade in your identity in order to conform.
- ✓ You've had setbacks yet want to leave your mark and be the difference that makes the difference.
- ✓ You want to thrive – and you don't want to lose any more time getting to that point.
- ✓ You're wondering whether it's you or someone else driving your life and are ready to live on your terms and feel free.
- ✓ You're someone who doesn't want to settle for someone else's agenda or conform to life's rules.
- ✓ You are ready to reclaim your inner balance.

If you can see yourself in any of those descriptions, you're going to love this book. You're someone who's ready to choose the way you want your life to be, making different decisions and with that changing your destiny and your results.

How to get the most out of this book

- ✓ You'll get the most out of this book if you interact with it by drawing pictures and writing notes and underlining the parts you want to come back to.
- ✓ Within each chapter, I have listed some Empowering Actions you can take to deepen your learning and experience of the techniques described in the book.
- ✓ At the end of each chapter, you will find some Zesty Takeaways. These are simple summaries of up what has been covered. You can use these as quick reminders of what you've read.
- ✓ Take time to reflect on what you read as you go along, and most importantly, have fun with it!

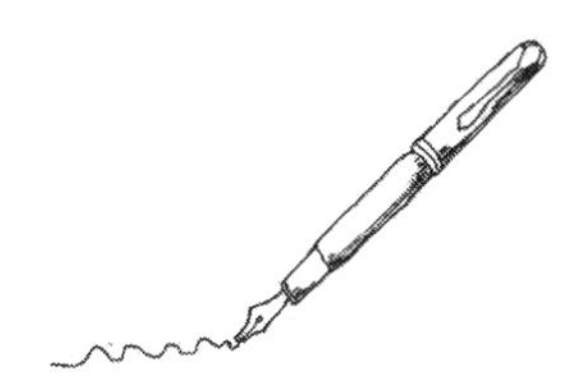

One thing is for sure, the only way to change your experience of life is to do something different. And this book will show you what to do differently, so you can begin to live a life that's authentic to you.

Get the FREE guide *The 11 Pillars of Balance* at https://www.marinazestforlife.com/balance-giveaway

PART ONE

WELCOME TO MY KITCHEN

My kitchen is the heart and soul of my home. It's where my day begins and ends, and where I spend most of my waking hours.

My mum's kitchen back at home in Spain is the same; it's where everything happens: we cry, laugh, talk and put the world to rights. We plan dinner (even though we've just finished lunch) and our special winter holiday menu (despite the fact that summer is just beginning).

Kitchens all around the world give us the perfect space for socialising and spending time with our loved-ones. It can be the heart of every home. For me, it's also the place where I meet my clients.

As you begin reading this book, I want you to imagine a friend has recommended that you come to see me and you've just stepped into my kitchen to begin your first session. I will give you the support and guidance you need to reclaim your story, inner freedom and joy in life. I want to help you become excellent at being *you*.

Today my warm, safe kitchen is yours. I'm excited that you're here because I know your life is about to go in a new direction as you change your habits and broaden your thinking. Your new journey is about to begin. As we start our first session, you tell me how you have lost the balance in your life and how nothing feels fun anymore.

"I've forgotten what it's like to feel joy," you tell me. "I feel distracted and lost, as if I'm going round in circles."

Although I've heard this before from others, your story resonates deeply with me.

"It's time to wake up and regain your inner balance," I tell you. "Your life is passing you by and there's not a moment to lose. Let's get started!"

And so our work together begins…

When the mind is in balance,
joy follows like a shadow that never leaves.

Buddha

Chapter 1

Falling Asleep at the Wheel

You have arrived early for our second session together and I can see you sitting outside in your car.

"I'll put the kettle on and get the coffee ready," I say to myself as I begin to get everything together.

Before I know it, you're ringing the doorbell and our session is starting.

"I realised something important a few days after I saw you" you tell me. "I realise I've been asleep at the wheel. I've stopped driving my life and I've stopped being me. I'm no longer present in my own life and I've given away my freedom."

I explain that many of us are so concerned about living life in a certain way that we lose our passion and give in to the pressure to be what others want us to be rather than being ourselves. We spend hours planning, planning, planning because we're terrified of making mistakes and being judged. As a result, there's no room for spontaneity in our lives anymore.

I know how easy it is for this to happen.

Several years ago, I wrote a different version of this book. But when I passed it to a friend, instead of telling me how great it was, she said, "You need to start again, Marina. This book isn't you."

She asked me whether the book made me smile (it didn't), whether it made me feel passionate and playful (it didn't) and whether it would help others change the way they lived (it wouldn't). She told me, "You're all about living life with joy and being true to yourself. This book doesn't send that message. Write the book that shares *your* message. Be yourself, Marina."

I was petrified. My heart was beating like a drum. Had I forgotten who I was? How could I not be myself in my own book?

Driving the car called life

We're all driving this magnificent car called life. It runs smoothly until we stop paying attention to where it's going. Almost without noticing, we get into a routine in our lives and fall into a sort of emotional paralysis. Eventually, we fall asleep at the wheel and stop being present in our lives at all. Sometimes, we even move over to the passenger seat and let someone else drive our car.

My friend had done me a huge favour. I had been writing my book sitting in the passenger seat of my life. I thought I was driving, but I wasn't. It was time for me to practise what I preach, walk the talk and be who I was meant to be.

So, as you can see, **it happens to us all at one time or another**. It doesn't matter how self-aware you are, you can still get distracted and find you've fallen asleep at the wheel. Self-awareness is about consciously knowing, understanding and being in touch with our motivation, emotions and desires – it enables us to take responsibility for our lives.

But rather than leap into action, I put off rewriting my book.

It wasn't until I was walking across London Bridge one day that everything changed. I happened to pass a bookshop and there in the window was my book! It had the same title as my book and the cover I'd imagined for it. Of course, it wasn't my book because I hadn't written it. Someone else had. So, there it was before my eyes, ready to dazzle the world. Life was telling me something. It said, "Listen, Marina."

I bought that book and I read it while I was on the train home. I was hoping it wouldn't be any good, but this book was brilliant. Oh my… I needed a strong gin and tonic! When I got home, I was too upset to eat, so I took my daughter's Chocolate Orange and ate the whole thing. It felt good to do something bad… and with my mouth full of chocolate and a mischievous grin on my face, I fell asleep.

Did I consider giving up? Well, yes. But only briefly. In the morning I got up, straightened my crown and said with solemnity, "I drive my life, so I decide what to do. The real power is in not giving up, Marina." And with that, I left my frustration and sorrow behind and set myself the mission of writing my book again.

That's my story and in it there is a message for you: that it is *you* who drives your life. So, I'm here to ask you what kind of journey you want to go on? Where do you want to go and what would you like to be written on your tombstone at the end of your journey?

The good news is that it doesn't matter whether the journey so far has been what you wanted. You can change direction, choose a new destination and create a life that inspires you. **Your job is to figure out what it looks like**. And I'll be by your side to guide you.

Reflections

Imagine what the very best version of your life looks like. Using the questions below to get you thinking, write your answers in your journal and explore your ideas more freely.

- What are you doing?
- Who are you doing it with?
- How does it make you feel?
- How are you living your life now and does it match the way you want it to be?
- What habits are you prepared to change so you can have the life you dream of having?
- How are you going to respond when things don't go to plan?

Not sure what that life looks like? Be patient, you have the whole book to find out. Life can take many twists and turns. So, to live a balanced life, it's important to be flexible, stay present and embrace everything that happens – that means the downs as well as the ups. No matter what comes along, you need flexibility to pick yourself up, dust yourself off and start all over again, and again, and again.

You're going to change the direction in which your life is going; it's time to start driving your life again. No matter what's gone before, it's never too late to live life on your terms, fully aware of the journey you're on. Take the risk of being seen and never settle for second best. **Make the story about you, not what other people expect or want from you. This is what being true to yourself is all about.** You are the driver; you are the one that chooses the journey and now is the perfect time to get out your map and plan a new route for yourself.

Empowering Actions

Create an environment of learning and calm every time you sit down to read this book. Make time to do the centring meditation below. It's designed to relax and balance you. It only takes a few minutes, though you can do it for longer if you wish.

- Close your eyes and breathe slowly until you feel relaxed. Imagine you're breathing through your heart.
- As you breathe, notice any emotions and connections that come up in or around your heart.
- Notice your heart energy expanding throughout your whole body.
- Allow your breath to return to your natural rhythm and when you're ready, open your eyes.

Zesty Takeaways

- ♥ Awareness and presence are the foundation of a balanced life.
- ♥ It's okay to feel defeated for a while, but it's not okay to give up.
- ♥ Jump in the driving seat of your life now, don't wait for a tragedy to wake you up!
- ♥ If you don't live your life being true to yourself *now*, when will you ever do it?
- ♥ **Now is always the perfect time to change the direction of your life.**

Chapter 2

Who is *Really* in Charge?

You're sitting at my kitchen table while I pour the coffee. You're talking about our last session and the meditation we did together.

"I loved the meditation we did last time," you tell me. "Though, I'm not sure whether my mind was making everything up or my body was responding to my emotions. Sometimes, I don't know which part of me is taking the lead, and that feels overwhelming."

The mind-body connection

I explain to you that the mind and body are part of the same system, and that everything is connected. Whatever affects your mind affects your body too. When your mind, body and soul are unified, it is as if they're one and they speak to you with one voice. When all three are in balance your life is in balance too.

We each have:

- A body that carries us everywhere and keeps us alive. It is our physical representative.

- A soul (consciousness) which is our inner life or inner intelligence. The soul gives us an awareness of our internal and external existence and is the essence of our being.
- A mind where our thoughts are created. Within the mind we have:
  - A conscious mind – which gives us the capacity to process mentally and think. Our conscious mind enables us to interpret our reality and bring it into our awareness. We make decisions from our conscious awareness.
  - An unconscious mind – which allows us to process thoughts, feelings and ideas that are outside our conscious awareness. It influences our decisions and behaviours but in a way we're not aware of.

If we want to change a negative thought, we bring it to our conscious mind first. This is when meditation can help as it opens a space for us to truly listen to ourselves.

Often in our daily lives we don't know which part of us we're listening to and this causes us internal conflict. **Awareness of which part of you is in charge of your actions is key to enabling you to lead your life the way you want to live it, in balance, and free from fear.** To achieve greatness, you must listen to your body, your inner intelligence, your values and who you are. And with what you discover, you can choose the thoughts that support the life you want to live.

You might think it's too much for you to pay attention all the time, yet it's not so hard. It's a bit like when you learn to drive a car. At the beginning, you think there's too much going on: the steering, speed, gears and then the other cars around you and the road signs. Arrrgggh! Too much!

And yet, after you learn and practice it's amazing how easy it gets. You no longer have to think about every move because it becomes second nature. You know exactly which gear you need, how fast to go and how to drive safely in traffic. It's the same with getting to know yourself and learning who is leading your life. When you're aware and clear about which part of you is leading, you become an experienced driver, in this case the expert driver of your own life. The more you notice and listen, the smoother life becomes.

The circles in your mind

It's easy for us to get stuck in our heads, thinking, thinking, thinking. Before we know it, we've lost sight of whether it's our deeper, more knowing self we're listening to, or a more judgemental and critical voice that's been constructed from our logical, socialised selves. Fortunately, practising self-awareness and inner observation separates the two and gives you clarity around the decisions you make.

Of course, I know it's easier said than done. The demands of everyday life require us to be constantly in our heads, thinking and processing logically. When that happens, we disconnect from our deeper selves and soon we no longer feel like our true selves. It's exhausting to live like this and it's no wonder we feel tired and stressed much of the time.

It's normal for most of us to have conversations with ourselves constantly running through our minds. You might recognise some of your own internal dialogue when reading the examples below:

"I need to introduce a new company policy to my team, even though I don't agree with it... I guess I'll just have to get on with it because I don't want to upset my boss. It feels all wrong to me, but I'll just have to go along with it. I'm upset with myself for going along with it. Why am I letting my head convince me I must do this when my intuition is telling me it doesn't feel right?"

"I disagree with what Claire is saying about what John did, but I won't say anything in case she thinks I'm being petty. I know I need to confront her, but I want to avoid an argument, even if it means I don't stand up for what I believe. I feel out of alignment with my values and I can physically feel this in my body. I just can't win."

Most of us know this can go on for days on end, wearing us down until we finally give in, and do what's expected of us, even when we know deep inside it's not congruent with who we are or what we think and feel. As a result, we end up feeling pulled apart, like a child being asked to choose between mum or dad.

Whenever you feel like this, stop and ask yourself what all this negative chatter is about and what's really going on. It's a sign that something important to you has been compromised, so listen. Take a moment to reset your thinking and avoid going round in circles.

Reset your thinking

To begin the process of resetting, make space to listen to what you really want, remember who you are and what is important to you regardless of what's going on around you. Refocus on where you were going before your negative chatter took over, so you can understand how you got to that mental space and why you took that detour. Doing this supports you in identifying what is not congruent with you and no longer works or serves you. And when you squash that negative voice and start listening to the positive messages instead, the results will be exhilarating. This level of self-awareness gives you true clarity. Somebody said that life is a balancing act, and so it is. **When in balance, your thoughts, emotions and physical responses are all in harmony**, giving you a sense of wellbeing that makes it easier to make decisions, deal with difficulties and enjoy life.

Alice, my client and friend, is a strong, independent woman. We had been working together for some time. She was flourishing and her life was moving in the direction she wanted it to go. One day, I asked Alice for a testimonial to use on my website.

This was her reply: "I'm more than happy to write you a testimonial, but can you give me an idea of what you'd like me to focus on? Do you want me to focus on the result, your unique way of working or the way you help your clients through various stages of the process? Do you want it to be a paragraph or three sentences? Do you want something you can use as a quote or more like a case study? Sorry to ask so many questions, but it makes things easier if I have an idea of what you want the testimonial to say or communicate."

My goodness, and all I was looking for was a simple testimonial. Why do we complicate everything to such an extent that we lose the joy and fun from what we do? Are us human beings difficult to please? No, we are not. We are just easily led and conditioned. We never cease to be the child who gets influenced by others, shiny things, and fast cars. As we grow older, material possessions might not influence us as they did. But we're still influenced by our environment, the behaviour of others and our thoughts, which sometimes behave like a naughty friend who wants to get us into trouble. When we get caught up in our head, we forget everything we've learnt, which is why inner observation is so important.

I could see that Alice was over-thinking the testimonial. I felt tired just reading her message, so I can only imagine how tired she must have felt at the end of each day listening to the chatter in her head all day long. I could sense the agitation in her message; her need to do well and her desire to give me the perfect testimonial when all I wanted was a few words written from her heart!

Alice's anxiety about doing what was required was the result of the pressure to always be on top of her game in a world of high expectations. When answering this simple question, she was responding straight from her head and not listening to herself. She had disconnected from the essential source of herself. Trapped in her thoughts, her conscious mind was the one dictating the message, typing away without questioning what she was saying. She forgot that it was she who drives her life; that she is not just made up of her mind and body – she's also her inner essence, an intelligence that can't be seen yet is unquestionably there.

I explained to Alice about the connection between mind, body and soul and said, "Don't think about anything specific. Explore your journey working with me and let those words speak out. How was it for you working with me? How is your life different now? Write it down and see what happens. Whatever comes out will be perfect."

She then wrote the most beautiful testimonial. She told me, "These ideas are really thought-provoking. It makes sense that everything is linked: mind, body and soul; I've noticed that it's worth paying attention because each one affects the others."

Change your thoughts

What happened to Alice, happens to us all. We lose ourselves in thoughts and forget which part of us is talking, acting, and driving our lives. It is a matter of grasping the idea and then becoming aware of which part of you is the one doing all these things: your mind, your body or your soul. Hopefully they are all in sync and work like a good team. With practice and observation, you'll soon be able to distinguish between each and choose who needs to be in charge when you're making a decision.

I encourage you to observe your thoughts and change them if you need to, because when you change what you think, you change your perspective and perception of the world. In turn, by doing that, you'll be able to alter your course and your destination. In the morning before you get dressed, pay attention to what you're thinking and if you don't like it, intentionally choose new thoughts. These thoughts create your feelings, and your feelings create your actions, and these actions create your reality. Your quality of life depends very much on your initial thoughts. So, think of a life full of zest and balance. Very simply, if you want a better life, think better thoughts.

You can think of it like this:

- Mediocre thoughts lead to mediocre feelings.
- Mediocre feelings lead to mediocre actions.
- Mediocre actions lead to a mediocre (or even a bad) reality.

So, if you don't like what you're experiencing, choose better thoughts, because:

- Extraordinary thoughts lead to extraordinary feelings.
- Extraordinary feelings lead to extraordinary actions.
- Extraordinary actions lead to an extraordinary life.

When you observe what you're thinking, you raise your self-awareness, becoming conscious of your capacity to choose, which allows you to gain confidence and move forward with clarity of mind. **Being clear about what you want from your life is crucial** as it gives you the power to make the best decisions for you. It allows you to form a plan and give yourself a clear destination and a route to getting there. That means you can take extraordinary action and drive your life in any direction and to any destination you choose.

When we live a life driven by our values, choices and awareness, we feel confident, powerful and full of zest.

Empowering Actions

How to tap into your mind, body and soul, and learn how to differentiate which is in control.

Step 1

✎ Go back and do the meditation on page 20. As you do so, observe your inner chatter and the messages coming from your body. Also, pay attention to the deeper 'something else' underneath all this that is purely you. It's the part of you that can't be seen but you know is there; an inner intelligence that gives your life congruence and balance. This is where the magic happens and how you access your inner wisdom. Remember, you are powerful, much more so than you ever imagined. Take your time and repeat it if necessary.

Take at least three deep breaths. Hold the image of yourself holding an orange balloon. As you breathe in, the air is full of joy and zest around you. As you breathe out, release what isn't serving you anymore and let go of the balloon at the same time. Explore any feelings, sounds or sensations that come up.

Step 2

Explore your answers to the question: **What would a life full of joy look and feel like to you?** Before you write anything in your journal, read the question a few times to get your imagination and intuition moving. Close your eyes so you can envision your answer or explore with more of your senses. As you write, add details like feelings, tastes, smells, sounds and anything else that makes it truly joyful for you.

Enjoy what happens when you give yourself permission to connect with your deeper self. If you can't envision an image of a joyful life at first, meditate again to shift your thinking and access your creative mind. As you meditate, trust that you can envision your joyful future and explore what comes to mind. Be patient.

If you take one thing away with you today, take this: the negative chatter in your head isn't in charge, you have access to an inner intelligence and greater wisdom, so listen to the deeper 'you', the essence of who you are, and start to take charge of your life. **When you change your thoughts, you change your perspective, your feelings and your actions and with that your world.**

"I keep six honest serving men
They taught me all I knew.
Their names are what and why and when
And how and where and who."

Rudyard Kipling

Zesty Takeaways

- ♥ You have access to an inner intelligence and higher wisdom, listen to it.
- ♥ Keep it simple and live your life authentically.
- ♥ Add joy and fun to your life plan.
- ♥ When you notice your thoughts going round in circles, stop. Give yourself some time and space, then restart.
- ♥ When your mind, body and soul are aligned, you change your experience of life.

Chapter 3

In Tune With Intuition

As I make the coffee, you tell me about a time when you listened to your intuition. "My intuition was telling me something was going to happen", you say, "and I listened."

"It was when I returned to work after a break. As I sat in my office, I heard something telling me this place was not for me anymore. It said I had to leave and find the place where I belonged. I didn't have another job to go to or any idea as to how I was going to earn money. I talked with my friends and family and they told me I was crazy to leave a reliable job, so I tried to ignore that voice. A few days later, I woke with a song in my head and I knew that a voice from inside was talking to me again. It was telling me to face my fears, move on and go back to college."

"What did it feel like?" I ask you.

"Well," you say, "I had an unusual sense of calm and certainty. I gave in my notice at work and left feeling sure that what I was leaving behind needed to go."

"What happened next?"

"I sat down on my own and asked myself what I really wanted. And the answer came to me loud and clear. I wanted to be a tutor and mentor. Not long afterwards, and while I was still studying, the phone rang and I was offered the job of my dreams, teaching psychology."

As you sit and reflect on this, the coffee brews and wraps its rich aromas around the kitchen. I ask if you'd like sugar in your coffee today. I notice how alive you are, as if a light bulb has been switched on. Everything seems to click, and I can tell you're back in that moment in time when everything came together.

"Looking back, who was driving your life then?" I ask.

Almost as if you're talking to yourself, you say, "My intuition was driving back then. I didn't listen to my head. I've heard my intuition speaking to me many times before and I chose to ignore it, now I know to follow it. But there was a time when I didn't listen to my intuition. It was when a friend introduced me to someone she was planning to go into business with. I didn't like this person and told my friend so, but she trusted him. I tried to like him for her sake, but I just couldn't. One day, she told me he'd been embezzling money from the business and at that point, I knew my intuition had been right."

"Now that you know what happens when you do and don't listen to your intuition, let's explore the difference it makes in your life and how you can tune into it more often," I say.

Your intuition is a magnificent navigation system that helps you make decisions from your heart rather than your head. It's always there, you just need to learn how to listen to it. When you do, you become hyper-aware of it.

Intuition means "to contemplate" or "to look within". It's an inner knowing that can't be explained with reason or logic. It's like the voice of your soul; wisdom that doesn't use words to communicate.

> *"The intuitive mind is a sacred gift, and the rational mind is a faithful servant.*
> *We have created a society that honours the servant and has forgotten the gift."*
>
> Steve Jobs

How listening to your intuition helps

Living a good life is an art and part of that is learning how to listen to your intuition. When you listen to your intuition, you make the most of what life has to offer because you make better decisions. You choose what's best for you and helps you feel at ease with yourself and your circumstances. Fortunately, your intuition is always talking to you; the only problem is that (most of the time) you're not listening. Or at least, you haven't learned *how* to listen.

Suzana Herculano-Houzel, a neuroscientist from Vanderbilt University, became famous for turning brains into soup. When she analysed that 'soup', she discovered that we have 86 billion neurons in our brain. Our thinking mind is made of:

- Prefrontal cortex (responsible for decision making.)
- Primitive brain (in charge of detecting threats.)
- Limbic (which hold the history of our emotional experiences.)
- Neocortex (where we store knowledge and basic thinking.)

The human brain has an incredible capacity to store and process data. And yet despite this, scientists are discovering that our intuitive mind is faster at making decisions than our thinking mind. In other words, we intuitively know the answers before our logical mind has assessed the situation and made a choice.

That's why listening to your intuition really matters. Dr Kelly Turner, a researcher and lecturer in the field of integrative oncology, did a piece of research that revealed how in almost every instance of radical remission from cancer, the patients used their intuition to help them make better decisions related to healing. (See page 188 for more information.)

When you have a major life decision to make, such us changing your career, deciding who to marry or where to live, and you don't know what to do, it's important to know that the feeling in your heart is *always* right. That gentle knowing, when listened to, leads to better outcomes in life. It's like an inner superpower that opens up possibilities and empowers you to act and do amazing things.

Logic comes from our conscious thinking mind and is ideal for making day-to-day decisions. When you feel conflicted or can't decide what you really want or what would make you happiest, explore and listen with your intuitive mind to dissipate any doubts. The answer that comes from your subconscious mind and inner knowing, doesn't come with doubts and indecision as the thinking mind does. It just has clarity.

Balanced living is all about making the most of life by living in the present. When we live in the present moment we take the world lightly, and that's at the heart of a joyful life. So, being in touch with your intuition brings you closer to the life you want to live. It means you can live a freer, zestier and more fulfilling life, making confident choices around anything from a new business idea to a new love. When you trust your intuition, you do more of what you want to do and get more of what you love.

Tune in to your intuition

We all have intuition; it's an intrinsic part of us. We don't have to learn how to use it, it simply evolves as we live. However, some people are more tuned-in to their intuition than others, and that's mainly because they practise listening for it and learn how to recognise it. To be more aware of your intuition, you need to strengthen your listening skills. It's a bit like watching the sun rise. You don't want to miss it, so you focus on the moment and allow yourself to simply be there, taking it all in.

There are many ways that your intuition communicates with you. For example, you might become aware of 'signs', such as flashing images, natural events or adverts that somehow talk to you. You may get goosebumps over a part of your body or hear a distinctive voice inside at particular and significant times. Or it might come to you as a soft whisper. It's different for everyone. If you feel agitated or anxious, it's your thinking mind you're hearing. When the communication comes from your intuition, you'll feel confident, calm and clear.

"There is a voice that doesn't use words, listen."

Rumi

How do you tune in to your intuition?

There is nothing mysterious about your intuition, you can tune into it just as you do with a radio. We tend to use the rational, left-hand side of our brain most. To access your intuition, you have to plug into the right-hand, creative side of your brain. It broadcasts in a different frequency to your logical brain. Just as with any radio station, the more you listen to it the more familiar with it you become.

How to pay attention to your natural knowing

Tune in by tuning out. What do I mean by this? Get rid of all distractions. A head full of thoughts, a noisy environment and stress won't help you to tune into your intuition. Move yourself from conscious thinking by doing something physical, meditating, walking in silence or doing something creative. These kinds of activities allow you to be present, which allows your intuition to come through. In other words, if you want to tune in, you need to tune out. When you're present, be curious like a child and listen with your whole body. Notice physical sensations and anything new around you. Ask for guidance and write down any 'aha' moments. The voice might not come when you ask it to, and you may notice it the following day as you wake or are doing something routine.

Is it your head or your intuition talking?

Most of us have been trained to listen to our conscious thoughts and logic, so first you need to let go of control and learn to trust your instinctive feeling. When making decisions using your intuition, you experience a level of certainty you don't always get with a logical decision. Somehow, there's an inner knowing and calm. You feel light and clear and you don't need to rationalise or justify your decision, you just know it's right. It's a very different experience to when you get stuck in your head. When that happens, fear kicks in, your body tenses, there's a lot of inner chatter and you feel agitated, lost in thought and unable to decide. When you get stuck in your head, remind yourself that this is not the energy that's going to help you. Get out of that space and practise mindful presence.

To be clear, I'm not telling you to ignore your rational and logical thinking. I'm saying listen to both your intuitive mind and your thinking mind before making a decision.

Is trusting your intuition risky?

Whenever you decide something, there is a risk attached. But there's no more risk in following your intuition than in trusting your logical mind. In fact, it's probably safer to trust your intuition and, in my opinion, it's worth the risk. At least when following your intuition, you are guaranteed an adventure and there is no adventure without learning!

Judgment or intuition

How do you learn how to distinguish judgment from intuition? The thing with intuition is that it doesn't matter how the person or thing comes to you, it will always give you the same signals consistently.

When you meet someone new, you probably make a lot of initial judgements about them. For example, you might decide you don't like them because of their voice or you may disagree with something they say. Maybe you simply don't like the way they're dressed. This is your mind judging and misleading you with preconceived ideas.

The next time you meet someone new, rather than trusting your initial impressions of them, listen and watch for how your body reacts instead. You might discover that they have a great energy. After that, it won't matter how many times you meet that person, you'll always respond to their energy. This is how I ended up in the UK, by listening to my intuition.

Intuitive decisions

When I was 25, I lived in Granada, Spain. I had a reliable job, friends and my loving family around me. There was absolutely no reason for me to change anything. Yet, one morning, I woke up and heard a voice telling me to go to the UK. It was a crazy idea, so I shook my head a few times and persuaded myself to ignore it.

For a while, I carried on as normal. I went out with my friends and kept myself busy doing lots of different things. But I couldn't ignore the voice – it was adamant it was going to be heard. I couldn't sleep for days, I felt unsettled and all wrong, and the voice kept coming back again and again. Then one day, I heard myself saying out loud to an empty room, "I'm leaving for the UK in a week."

I bought the plane ticket immediately and only told my parents about it the next day. As you can imagine, it didn't go down very well. They were shocked and unhappy about my decision. Worried, they asked me where I was going to live, how long I was going for, how I was going to earn money. All I could tell them was that two of my girlfriends were living there and that I trusted I could figure out the rest.

For some reason, their questions and fears didn't affect me. My intuition was so strong, it was all I could hear. It was urgently and fiercely directing me to go to the UK. So, I agreed with my family that I would return home in six months. And so, I left to live in this tiny loft in London, where my friends were living. I couldn't speak

English and I didn't have a plan. I simply followed my intuition, stayed curious and trusted myself.

Although London was my first stop, I knew instantly that I wasn't meant to live there. My head was telling me I should go home but I was enjoying myself, so I was in no rush to leave. I persisted and a year later, I heard the same voice again. "Time to move, explore and learn. This is not the place."

I had no idea where this voice came from! It seemed to come from within me. My head was telling me to go back to Spain, but that clear and undeniable voice inside me was directing me elsewhere. A few days later, I headed to Victoria railway station in London with just a small rucksack.

I was in the queue waiting to buy a ticket. I wanted to go somewhere nice, but I didn't know where. The woman in front of me asked for "a single ticket to Brighton, please." Next, it was my turn and what came out of my mouth was, "a single ticket to Brighton, please."

I was amazed. I didn't ask for information about any other cities or take the time to make a calculated and analytical decision. I tried to listen to my head, but I had the same feeling in my body as when I decided to come to the UK, and I knew it wouldn't leave me alone. So, I went with it. I was going to follow my intuition again. Ten minutes later, I left London for Brighton.

Once in Brighton, something inside me said, "I'm going to live here." What? Where did that thought come from? Was that a thought or a voice? I hadn't even explored the city yet! Besides, I'd promised my parents I'd stay with my girlfriends, though I'd already broken the promise of going home after six months.

It was too late. I listened and followed the trail; I had no time for regrets. I couldn't explain this feeling. It was as if I was making the decision with no reference to logic. In fact, it felt as if it was made by something bigger than me, and yet I was calm and confident, fully trusting myself.

This is the process I went through.

"I have to follow that call," I said.

But my inner world was now very much alive and talking back to me.

"And what if...?" Doubt said.

"Bad things will happen," Fear warned.

"I can handle it," said Trust.

"If you don't believe in me, who will?" replied my inner self, fully awakened now.

"Trust always. Trust in me," I demanded, "I am the driver on this journey."

And with the certainty of someone who knows something life changing is about to happen, I decided to stay. It was 1999, and after just a week in Brighton, I met the man who was to become my husband. I now know following that call was the best thing I ever did.

Intuition feels like a high vibration in your soul: positive energy. Your intuition shows you the path and your cognitive brain allows you to explore it. If you believe it, you will see it; all you need to do is trust that it's there.

I'm glad to say that my intuition is still alive and well – and it's never let me down. In fact, it's stronger than ever and I've had many amazing adventures as a result, and all of them have ended well. Don't get me wrong, I've made as many mistakes as the next person, but these mistakes were the result of decisions I'd made when I'd chosen to ignore my intuition. The signs are always there. My hair standing on end, a whisper, a loud voice. That feeling of 'don't get in the car with that person', 'follow that job', 'make that call'. The knowing in your heart. Does this ring any bells for you?

So, how do you make this work on a practical level when your mind is full of noise? Well, first set the intention of listening to your intuition. Next, create space in your mind to hear it, allow time to listen to it and gain perspective on everything it says to you. You can do this through meditation, mindfulness or simply taking a walk. Be willing to learn, be curious and allow whatever happens to happen.

"When your head says, 'Yes,'
and your heart says, 'Yes,'
but your gut says, 'No!'
Be wary. Be wise."

Marleen Woolgar

Empowering Actions

I invite you to do something with me; we are going to breathe. Don't worry we'll take it slowly and I will count for you as well.

Step 1

- Breathe in for a count of four, hold for four and breathe slowly out to the count of six. Repeat four times.

Step 2

- As you breathe, imagine you have a golden light coming through your head to your feet. Take time to do this, as it puts you in a state of presence which is an essential tool to listen to your intuition.

Step 3

- As you finish, open your eyes and listen: observe what happens around you and explore the silence in your mind.

Step 4

- To turn this intuitive conversation into something more tangible, take a journal and write something without thinking. Let the pen go where it wants to go and you'll be surprised by what you write, all it takes is a few minutes to centre yourself.

By now, you can probably remember many times when your intuition was talking to you or was showing you the way and you weren't aware of it. Perhaps everything is becoming clear now and you can see how the answers were always inside you. Now that you know this, you can decide where you drive to in your life, and with whom.

"Not everything that can be counted, counts, and not everything that counts can be counted."

Albert Einstein

Zesty Takeaways

- Intuition is an inner knowing and the voice of your soul.
- Intuition is that thing you can't touch or see and yet you know it is there.
- Intuition feels calm, safe and clear. It has certainty in it.
- Energy never lies, words do.
- **Trust your intuition!**

Chapter 4

The Power of Self-Love

It's lunchtime, so I offer you something to eat and you love the idea. We begin to talk about the previous session and the changes you want to make.

"How do I find the time to make these changes when I'm so busy with family, work, home and friends?", you ask me.

"By setting yourself free and loving yourself." I reply.

"I don't know if I can," you say.

"It takes love, especially self-love; nothing good happens without it," I say.

Now, ask yourself how important your life is to you and how much you love and value yourself. If you don't feel worthy or that your life isn't the most important life in the universe or that you're not loveable enough, it's time to find out why and how you arrived at this point.

Whether it's self-love or love for others, love requires a profound and unconditional acceptance; no ifs and no buts. You might find it easier to love others than yourself and when it comes to loving yourself, you may feel some resistance. So, let's explore this a bit further.

Self-Care

This is the kind of love that supports us to achieve, connect with others and thrive.

> *"Give the ones you love wings to fly,*
> *Roots to come back and reasons to stay."*
> The Dalai Lama

I often reflect on these words because they remind me that when we love unconditionally and without expectation, we set those we love free to be themselves and live their life as they want to live it. If we love ourselves in the same way, we give ourselves the same freedom. The aim is to have a balanced life, and nobody is going to hand it to you on a plate. You are the one who creates your life; avoiding risk and discomfort isn't going to give you memorable and enjoyable experiences.

I heard a story from a teacher about a boy she taught. This boy told her how back in his village in Colombia, new born babies are presented with a piece of cane to remind them to stay on a straight path throughout their life. Every year, on his birthday, this boy was given a new stick as a reminder. The straight path represents taking responsibility for his actions. I loved the wisdom in this story and the message that life doesn't just happen, we make it happen, and that we need to be reminded to do so with a good dose of care and love.

I often tell my clients I have a cane behind the door which I'll use if they don't wake up and start taking hold of the wheel and driving their lives. Funnily enough, they suddenly become excellent at looking after their own needs. When my clients and I remember that piece of cane, we stop asking someone else to take responsibility for our lives. I hope you remember it too! Caring about yourself is your responsibility and nobody else's.

A combination of love and care provides the foundations of a fulfilling life. So, if you're ever tempted to give up on yourself or your goals, ask yourself: How important is this to me? And if the answer is 'very important', keep working at it.

Recognise your strengths and weaknesses for what they are and then accept them. There are some things you can't change about yourself, like how tall you are or the fact that you love chocolate ice cream! Of course, there are things you can change, like how fit you are and how early you get up in the morning.

We're all different and some people think they are incapable of setting goals because they never know what they want. It's no surprise then that these people live directionless, unmotivated lives. They tend to blame life, their parents, their environment, their education and their background for their lack of success. They look at successful people and put their achievements down to the fact that *their* life has been easy. If only...

At the opposite end of the spectrum are the people who are too harsh on themselves. Their self-critical approach holds them back from taking risks or sorting out their lives, constantly sabotaging any chance of success. Instead, they focus on asking others to support their goals and aspirations. Yet all this achieves is lower self-esteem and an even more depleted sense of self-worth because all they do is convince themselves that they don't matter.

Eventually, they become bitter and angry because they feel used and invisible when they've created this situation themselves.

Let me introduce you to Sarah. She's the CEO of a large company and she has a brilliant mind. One of her strengths is that she can always see solutions rather than problems. This is one reason why she's so good at her job. Another is that she's great at spotting other people's strengths and developing them. Yet, when I told her how fantastic she is, she couldn't own it and found her own ability very hard to accept.

You might recognise yourself here, although if you do, don't worry, you're not the only person who struggles to accept compliments and indulges in self-critical thinking. It seems that giving praise is far easier than accepting it.

How is it that we find it so difficult to acknowledge our strengths? Is it because we think acknowledging our brilliance is boasting? Is it because being humble seems more acceptable than being confident? Whatever the reason, **you won't gain anything by holding yourself back for the benefit of others!** There's nothing to gain from this way of thinking. You're just robbing yourself and others of your talents. What's more, it takes you further from the life you want and can have, not closer.

We all know someone (or maybe you are that person) who is constantly questioning their ability, right up to the point where they sabotage their success, ensuring that their experience fits their narrative of being 'useless' or 'not good enough'. This is a sign that they've mastered the art of listening to their internal negative chatter and have forgotten how to listen to their hearts.

Empowering Actions

Ask yourself the following questions then write down what comes to mind.

- How important am I to myself?
- If I'm not that important, why not?
- What part of me am I still afraid to love and how can I change that so I can move on?
- What would my life be like if I loved myself? Imagine it…

Find some time to be on your own and allow the answers to these questions to come to you. It's easier for answers to come when you slow down and give yourself space to reflect. It doesn't matter what you do: you can cry, do something you enjoy, dance, be silly or laugh until your belly aches. It doesn't matter. As long as you look at yourself and accept who you are.

Care about yourself enough to get out of your comfort zone and become your best self. When you love yourself fiercely, it ensures you don't settle for less than you deserve. Take care not to push to the point where you feel exhausted – do your upmost to avoid that. Loving yourself sometimes means spoiling yourself or being alone and if you can't bear the thought of doing that, it might be a sign that something has to change.

Imagine what it would be like to be loved unconditionally for who you are and not what you do for others. If you haven't experienced that yet, work on loving yourself. Show up like a ferocious lion or lioness protecting its precious cubs, only this time it's *you* you're showing up for. Don't take life too seriously, ditch anything that weighs you down and set yourself free. You'll probably have to do this again and again as you grow and change, and as what you want changes too.

- Set yourself free by practising self-acceptance.
- Praise and compliment others often.
- Praise yourself daily!

If you want to thrive and change the world, you have to walk the talk.

"The mark of a wild heart is living out the paradox of love in our lives. It's the ability to be tough and tender, excited and scared, brave and afraid, all in the same moment. It is showing up in our vulnerability and our courage, being both fierce and kind."

Brené Brown

Accept yourself and others

Anthony came to me one day asking me for help with his daughter. He explained how she was always comparing herself to others and how she struggled to accept herself. Nothing was ever good enough for her and she blamed everyone else for her unhappiness. When taking her exams, she made her parents' life hell as she took out her anxieties and distress on them. Even though her results were good, they still weren't good enough for her.

Anthony told me how he and his wife did everything they could to make their daughter happy. They took her on holidays, bought her expensive clothes and gadgets, and indulged her with expensive meals. They took her to coaches, counsellors, doctors and psychologists, but somehow nothing worked. He asked me if there was anything I could do for his daughter. I explained that only self-love and acceptance would help her. And she needed to stop comparing herself to others.

He asked me how he could teach her this and I told him that although he could guide, support and advise her, this was something only she could do for herself. All the time she blamed others for her situation rather than taking responsibility for it, she wouldn't change. Ultimately, she was the only one who could help herself – and she could only do it when she was ready.

I told him that the day she realises she doesn't need to compare herself to anyone else, she'll stop resisting and start accepting herself for who she is. She'll find peace and start seeing rainbows where she once only saw rain.

I told him, "Stop trying to fix the situation or make her feel better. Allow her to make mistakes and put them right if she chooses. She needs the opportunity to discover she has the resources to change and that you can't and won't make everything okay for her. In time, she will realise she can handle anything and when that happens, she'll start to trust herself. If she finds it too much, she'll ask for help and support. It's her decision to do so, not yours. It might take her six months or it might take her 15 years. Your job is to be there when she needs love, that's all. Loving and accepting your daughter as she is right now is the best gift you can give her. Also, work on accepting and loving yourself as that'll help you to stop feeling you have to fix everything and rescue everybody."

Anthony clearly felt deflated when he heard this. It wasn't what he wanted to hear at all. There was a long silence, and you could have cut the air with a knife. Yet I sensed that the penny had finally dropped. He didn't like it, but he understood it.

The truth is that we can't accept others if we can't accept ourselves first. This caring father was trying to find a solution for his daughter; he was trying to treat the symptoms rather than dealing with the real reason for her behaviour and lack of joy. Of course he loved his daughter dearly, he was just conflicted as he had no idea what it meant to love someone else or himself unconditionally – to accept them as they are: human beings with flaws – and love them despite those flaws and without trying to fix them.

Fortunately, the story ended well. After reaching rock bottom, Anthony's daughter started exploring career avenues and fell in love with teaching. Once she found her purpose, she had meaning in her life and that drove her forward. She now teaches children how to accept and love themselves, no matter what.

The next time you feel tempted to fix someone, ask yourself, "What do I need to accept in myself first?"

None of us needs to be fixed. We need to be accepted. So, love people for who they are, not for what you want them to be. Have faith and trust that your loved ones will feel so loved and accepted by you that they'll have the confidence to fly, using their skills to create a life they love.

When we love ourselves, we make it easy for others to love us too.

You are enough

Every day, we're bombarded by media, social networks and people telling us we need to improve ourselves, to be more and do more. The list is endless, and it can make us feel as if we're never enough. As a result, balance goes out the window. Before we know it, we've convinced ourselves we're not lovable and we're not enough.

If you don't love yourself unconditionally, you can't expect others to love you unconditionally either. When you accept the person you see in the mirror, warts and all, you restore inner balance – the alignment of mind, body and soul – and then wonderful things start to happen.

When you know you are enough, regardless of what's been happening in your daily life, you feel safe and adequate; you have faith that everything will work out fine. You allow a more expansive version of yourself to shine out. Everything you do feels easier because there isn't any pressure to prove yourself. You know you are valued for who you are, not for what you do.

If you have children, tell them you love them and, no matter what they do, make them feel safe and wanted. It doesn't matter if they make you angry or disappoint you, tell them that nothing can change how you feel about them. Show some appreciation to your partner. Tell your friends you love them too. Even better, show them regardless of what they give back to you or what they've done, you will love them.

At home we have a gorgeous Cavachon, a cross between a Bichon Frise and a King Charles Spaniel. She's small and fluffy, so we called her Fluffy. She's got the personality of a cat, which means she minds her own business and does what she likes. She lies on the softest feather pillows and loves herself too much to come and say hello if she's tired.

At night, she sits with us for about three minutes before deciding we're annoying and wriggle too much. She simply gets up and goes to find the most comfortable place in the house. And she definitely does not go for a walk when she doesn't want to, not even if you drag her across the floor. She doesn't try to do anything to win our love, yet we adore her. Fluffy feels her presence is enough, she doesn't have to perform to earn her keep. She knows we want her just as she is.

Learn to love yourself

So, how do you learn to love yourself if you've never been taught? Begin by quietening your mind, choose one of the meditations in this book to help you. It's time to change your perspective and shift your thinking about love. Set aside what others have told you about self-love and start afresh, give yourself a chance to experience it. Relax, and allow life to unfold. Make a conscious effort to take life less seriously and explore what happens next. The next step is to accept who you are – and who you are not – flaws and all. Say out loud, "I am enough!" Don't worry when or if you feel awkward or feel yourself trying to resist the power of these words. Simply doing this exercise will make a difference. You've made a good start.

To make this work, say these words intentionally and as if you mean them – even better, mean them with all your heart. Connect the energy of love to the words you say, until you experience it. If you don't put any intention or emotion into your words, you'll just be repeating them like a parrot, copying sounds you hear without any feeling or understanding. When what you say doesn't mean anything to you, nothing changes because nothing in you has changed.

Repeat the "I am enough" phrase daily. Also, notice how you speak *to* yourself *about* yourself as well as to others. If you use negative language and tell yourself you're useless or berate yourself for making a mistake, you're just giving away your control. Believe it or not, words have more power than you imagine! It isn't just your mind listening, your body is listening too. So, don't let berating yourself become part of your identity. Right now, the only problem you have is believing you're not loveable. As you can see, one little sentence could change your life. So, keep saying with intention, "I am enough!"

You might think it's ridiculous or vain to love yourself, and when I first started to practice this, I was sceptical too. I didn't have much to lose though, so I kept going. It felt weird at the beginning and that's fine, weird is okay. I trusted, persisted and set the intention fiercely in my mind and heart until everything changed. I learned how positive these words were when I repeated them intentionally and with emotion. I noticed the impact language had on my body and the way I engaged with life. It was huge and far bigger than I thought it would be. As the way I spoke to myself and about myself changed, so my energy shifted. That's when the world around me transformed.

The truth is that nothing and nobody else can make you feel worthy if you don't accept yourself first. When it comes to self-love, we can't ask others to do for us that which we cannot do for ourselves. This is why we fall apart when others don't accept us. We are looking for acceptance and validation outside ourselves. We're looking for assurance from others that we are important and that we belong. **As long as you look outside to receive the love that only you can give to yourself, you will never be happy.**

It's possible your parents didn't tell you that you mattered at a time when you needed their reassurance, and it's possible they never will give you the validation you're looking for. So, ultimately, it's your responsibility to accept and love yourself, nobody else can do it for you. When you find yourself wanting to be accepted by others, remember that you must accept yourself first. **We can't expect others to love us, not even our parents. To love in a healthy manner, we must first learn to love ourselves.**

One day, a long-standing client told me, "I love me whatever happens. I have missed myself so much that I promise to always love and respect myself." He decided to love himself whatever happened in his life. When he finally accepted himself in this way, it was like sewing together the seams of a special outfit we had been creating together for months. It had taken him a long time to accept himself because he'd been constrained by the belief that unless he was successful every day, he wasn't enough. At the time, he was looking for love and recognition from his father, who never told him what he did was good enough. As a result, he was left feeling empty and undeserving. He couldn't allow himself to feel happy unless he'd achieved something every day, and even when he did, he never felt he'd done enough. Fortunately, on this particular day, the penny dropped and he finally understood that self-worth has nothing to do with what you've accomplished in a day. He had come to know that it was him who was driving his life, and that it was his choices that would take him in one direction or another. From that moment on he made the decision to choose himself over others.

For others to value you and see your worth, you first need to value yourself.

When you feel good about yourself, you know you matter and that your life has meaning. Even when others call you ugly names, you know your worth; you're strong. You don't need someone else to reassure you. Only unconditional self-love can give you validation because there are no strings attached to it. Loving yourself is like having a magic wand. You wave it and you experience acceptance, appreciation, and confidence. You can tell when someone loves themselves because they're full of life. They don't care what others think of them. These are the people who create awesome opportunities for themselves and others and know they deserve it. You can be that person too.

Keep saying 'I AM ENOUGH' intentionally and with emotion, no matter what you're doing and whether you're achieving great things or not. Even on a day when you haven't been at your best or don't feel you deserve to be loved, shout it out loud – it feels so good! It is empowering to say 'I love me!' Just give yourself a little kiss or a pat on the back and show yourself that *you* value *you*! Ridiculous? Well, most things are if you think about it.

What is the secret to achieving self-love? Doing it until you believe it and you become it. For love's sake, love your whole body, your awkward messiness, forgetfulness, and your mistakes. Love the fact that you don't know everything and don't know what tomorrow brings. Love your imperfectly perfect being and trust that whatever happens, you are enough.

"If I am not for myself, then who will be for me?
But when I am for myself, then what am 'I'?
And if not now, when?"

Rabbi Hillel

Empowering Actions

Let's play a little game.

Step 1

- Think of all the reasons why you love and appreciate yourself. For example, I love me even when I'm sad, angry and mad. I love me… (write as many examples as you can think of).

Step 2

- When you've done this, have a rest. Allow what you've learned in this chapter to sink in. Take a few deep breaths in and out, releasing any tension letting go, allowing yourself to be!

Zesty Takeaways

- Remind yourself often, "When I feel enough, everything is enough."
- "I am enough, whether I have achieved my goals or not."
- Words have power, so use them wisely.
- Being loved unconditionally allows you to live life to the full.
- Feel proud of even your tiniest achievements.
- Love yourself and others unconditionally, it's a love that speaks louder than words or actions.
- **When we love ourselves, we make it easy for others to love us back.**

Chapter 5

On Being Your Best Self

You arrive late, looking exhausted. This isn't like you, so I offer to make you a cup of tea and ask what's wrong.

"I'm so tired!" you blurt out. "My neighbour had a party last night. It was really noisy and went on until the early hours! It's just not normal to have a big party in the middle of the week like that!"

I smile and wonder 'what is normal?'

Yesterday, I was at a school teaching my teenagers' self-development programme. We pushed the tables and chairs aside and sat on the floor. When the bell rang for the next lesson, the next teacher came in and mentioned how unorthodox this way of teaching was. For him, it was not normal to see a class set up that way. He was uncomfortable because it wasn't something he was used to.

And what is normal? For most of us, 'normal' means behaving in a way that conforms to expectations. It's about fitting in and following established patterns. But it's just an idea. Most of us don't behave normally at all, so the only thing the idea of normal does is restrict us, clipping our wings and preventing us from living and achieving to our full potential.

We are tremendously influenced by how society defines normal and although at times we have to accept it, we don't need to conform all the time, especially if being 'normal' doesn't benefit anyone.

If you always try to conform, you'll never know how fantastic you can be.

Resist the urge to conform

I went to a traditional Spanish school run by nuns. As a country, we had emerged from 36 years of dictatorship. As a result of this oppressive regime, most people had put on a mental and emotional mantel of conformity.

This is why one particular nun called Concha had such a big impact on me. She was also my science teacher and my tutor. She was the only nun who didn't wear a habit or behave the way most nuns behaved.

Concha had jet-black, curly and very bushy hair and she wore thick glasses that made her eyes look huge and oval. Mostly, she wore a denim mini skirt with thick woolly tights and a pair of trendy flat shoes.

It wasn't just her appearance that was different; she talked differently too. She was as sharp as a razor and certainly didn't sugar-coat her language for us. That was a huge surprise!

Her courage in standing out fascinated me. She was like a regal owl in her own kingdom, proud of where she stood and had an energy and presence that made me notice her.

When us children asked her why she looked different and didn't do what the other teachers did, she explained that her job and commitment to God were both sacred to her and how her appearance and approach to teaching wasn't what made her either a good nun or a good person.

On fine days, she taught us outside on the patio (which wasn't normal at the time). Yet, when she did, there was magic in the air. The way she conducted the class made everyone want to learn so much more that even the daily church service became a moment of celebration.

Concha, often took her guitar along to mass and asked us to sit on the steps of the church. She encouraged everyone to sing, not just the children with good voices. Something changed when we were all included in this way. We felt validated and equal, part of something bigger than ourselves. The atmosphere was electrifying! We learned masses and had fun as well. Concha no doubt was the difference that made the difference to us. She celebrated herself and others as they were, and that's real power!

In a very politically and culturally sensitive time for Spain, she dared to go against the norm. How she got away with it, I don't know. What I do know is that by her being true to herself she touched the lives of hundreds of students, including me. She encouraged us to choose our own values over those of others. To be courageous enough to live our passion in spite of the fear of being labelled, and to celebrate our differences. Essentially, she showed us we could choose who we wanted to be.

Her last words to me were inspiring. She told me, "If you always conform, you'll never know how fantastic you can be." From that day on, I decided to be my true self and wear my skin with pride rather than trying to be like everyone else.

So, the next time you find yourself conforming, think again. Don't give up on what you want just to fit in with the crowd. Ask yourself: 'How is this helping me to thrive? Do I need to be like them and does this take me closer to being my best self?' And if not, ask yourself 'What would I like to have happen?' Take action and walk the talk, we can lie to others, but we can't lie to ourselves – at least not for long!

What is normal anyway?

Most of us nowadays have friends and clients who don't have a nine-to-five job. We know same-sex couples. Some of us or some of our friends have children without getting married. Others are bipolar, suffer from depression, autism, ADHD and other mental disorders from a very young age. For them this is their normality. If you saw them and did not know anything about them, they would look very normal, and that is because they are normal!

Now, if you found out their label, more likely than not, you would treat them differently or would think they are not normal; unfortunately it is what we have learned.

According to society, I am not normal. I laugh more than the norm and not necessarily at the most intelligent or funny things. I rarely watch TV, I have two breakfasts a day and I hate the smell of marijuana. I talk to everybody and my kids tell me I laugh too loud and I'm far too jolly and friendly. When I asked them why they thought so, they both said: "We live in a society where people don't talk or smile at each other, you can't act like this." I wondered how you could ever be too joyful. For a split second I contemplated conforming and being 'normal', but I knew deep down that conforming meant I would have to change not only how I behave, but also what I believe and value. To me, that meant letting others decide for me, which meant *they* would be driving my life, not *me*.

I realised I could lie to others, but I couldn't lie to myself. I knew what I wanted! I wanted to be happy, balanced and live a life true to myself. So, with the potential threat of disappointing my own children, I stood up for myself and trusted that they would soon see life from a different point of view. And fortunately, they did. Phew!

My personal view is that most people's 'normal' behaviour casts a shadow over the best version of themselves, sometimes even killing their creativity and their capacity to engage in life and all they stand for. Normality is different for everyone, so a change of perspective is often all that's needed for us to experience a different reality.

Fortunately, normal also changes, for instance: in Roman times it was normal for men to wear skirts, today apart from a couple of places in the world, it is not. It was normal to have slaves; today it is not normal, in fact it is illegal. It was normal to smoke in restaurants, not to pick up your dog's excrement and for women to stay at home rather than have a career.

Today none of these things are normal. All it took was a change in perspective to make something that was normal, not normal.

For some of us, it is normal to feel angry as well as sad, distressed, scared and stressed. As normal as it is for others to feel happy, content, at peace and in love. Unfortunately, when we feel rage, anger, distress and the other so-called negative feelings, we tend to suppress them as we have been told by the 'normal society' that it's not normal to show it, express it or even in certain circles admit these feelings exist.

We've all heard phrases like, 'boys don't cry', 'man up', 'pull yourself together', 'stiff upper lip', and 'you're too emotional'. Someone once even told me that I smile too much. What utter nonsense! I'm looking forward to the day when I hear people say that it's okay for boys to cry, that men don't have to 'man up', that it's acceptable to be vulnerable and that it's great to smile like a Cheshire cat.

I'm not asking you to follow my normal. Instead, I'm asking you to question yourself before you decide whether it sits right with you. If it doesn't, change it. Now, what would happen if you *only* followed your own needs and wishes? It would be great, wouldn't it? No, it wouldn't. You would probably end up in prison, isolated and very lonely and we don't do lonely well. We are the kind who need other people whether we like it or not and live in a society with rules for all.

Don't do it for others, do it for yourself and be your best self.

Empowering Actions

Step 1

The next time you're about to conform, ask yourself:

- Is their normal my normal?
- What *is* my normal?
- Does this 'normal' fit with my values and is it aligned with who I am and who I want to be?
- How could accepting their version of normal help me improve myself?
- What impact would I like to have on others? And is it the same as the impact I'm having right now when I'm following the herd?

Step 2

Think of someone who's inspired you in some way. What made that person different? What was it about them that inspired you and what made them stand out from the crowd?

Step 3

Draw a line down the middle of a piece of paper to make two columns. Label one column 'The Attributes of the Person I want to Be' and the other column 'The Attributes

I have Today'. Fill in the columns then compare the attributes of the person you want to be (your best self) with the person you are now, so you know what changes you need to make. By doing this, you can discover who you'd like to be or who your real self is.

For each version explore the questions below.

- How do you look and feel?
- What are you doing for a living?
- Who are the people close to you?
- What makes you want to be surrounded by them?
- How are you living life?
- How do you deal with the stresses of life when they happen? Because they do happen.
- How much do you love your life?

Step 4

When you look at where you are in comparison with where you want to be, you'll notice there's a gap between the two. So, if you want to get from A to B, you're going to have to change a few things.

Dig a bit deeper and, using the table below write down in the gap column what it is you have to do to become your better self. Focus on what will support you in achieving your goals.

Me Today	The Gap	The Best Version of Myself

When you reveal the gap, explore what changes are needed, while at the same time checking that your goal is congruent with who you are. This will allow you to plan what to do next. The next step is to **take action**. Without action there is no change and there are no results. The reward? Living a balanced life with meaning, joy and gratitude.

Step 5

Begin by writing down the first three actions you're going to take to create the change you want in your life. As soon as you achieve one of these actions, add another, until you become the person you want to be.

Keep questioning yourself so you explore what you want and what you enjoy. As you do this, you may have doubts – and others may raise doubts in your mind – this is fine. Remember you will only be congruent with yourself when you get to where you want to be.

Don't be ashamed of not having everything planned. Most incredible businesses came into existence with very little or no plan at all, just the willingness to have a go, play and have fun. "What if I make a mistake?" I hear you ask. If you make a mistake, reflect on what you needed to learn, integrate it and then start again; it's no big deal. When you fall, simply get up again and again, like a child learning to walk! As my teacher said, there is no failure, only feedback – and with that comes learning and progress. Living life this way supports you in being braver, more courageous, and perhaps even having more fun.

Choose who you want to be, whether normal or not and surprise yourself with a world of possibilities in front of you. As we embody who we are, we go from incongruent to congruent. **When we're in tune with our actions and emotions, life becomes simpler and more beautiful; balanced, because we're being true to ourselves.**

So, be bold, take risks and trust in yourself and the world around you. There is something very empowering about watching someone who's comfortable in their own skin; it's electrifying. Whenever you feel you're being put in the box and labelled 'not normal', celebrate; you are being yourself.

As we finish for the day, I show you a photo I took while strolling around the city I live in. It's a picture of the basketball court on Brighton seafront. On the front panel of the baskets, there is a big sign in dark purple and yellow that's impossible to miss. It reads: 'NEVER-NORMAL BRIGHTON'. It's wonderful to experience a city celebrating its differences with pride.

Then, with a sense of anticipation of what will happen in our next sessions, you are gone.

You are allowed to have doubts, you can even change your mind, but quitting when the road gets tough is not an option.

Zesty Takeaways

- Their normal might not be your normal; the decision to conform is a choice, so choose what's right for you.
- There is something very empowering about someone who's comfortable in their own skin.
- Celebrate your differences and those of others. That's real power.
- **Live your passion in spite of the labels.**

Chapter 6

Be Honest with Yourself

By now you are familiar with the routine when you arrive for your session. I get out the biscuits and plates while we wait for the kettle to boil, and we chat.

"Everything seems so perfect in this kitchen," you say.

"There is no such thing as perfection." I tell you. "Look at this dessert plate, for instance, it's a copy of a Wedgwood design. My fridge is broken, and I have been using the microwave as a bread bin for years. No matter how it looks, **we all have something fake or broken in our lives.**"

Then we start talking about self-honesty.

"I work so hard at having the perfect family, the perfect children and house and something always seems to go wrong. Then, I look at my friends… they look so happy, they have the perfect lives, the perfect kids," you say.

Perfect? Even if it's perfect for someone else, it might not be perfect for you. Most of our lives are far from perfect and if anyone denies it, they're either unaware or pretending.

What's more important than trying to be perfect is knowing that **life doesn't have to be perfect to be great.** We have perfect *moments* for sure, but most of the time, our life is far from perfect. Living is an adventure and like every good adventure it has its dark moments, its highs and lows. Waves of happiness and sadness, joy and stress radiate through our lives. This is what makes life so interesting. So, be curious and embrace your not-so-perfect life. **Often, when we free ourselves from the thought of having to have a perfect life, we end up loving the life we have right now. Just like a spring with no resistance, we relax.**

We are all different and deal with situations in our own ways. The intensity of our lives varies too. There are unresolved situations or emotions that are challenging to deal with. We can sweep the dust under the emotional carpet for a while. Then one day, the pile is so big, we trip on it and all our pent-up emotions rush out. It's as if a hurricane is sweeping through our lives, blowing our buried mess everywhere and shaking our whole world.

When that happens, we get overwhelmed by feelings because we're being forced from a deep, emotional sleep into awareness. That kind of wakeup call feels more like a slap, shocking us into realising we've lost our life balance. The version of ourselves we've been projecting onto the world conflicts with who we are and that leaves us feeling confused and out of alignment.

We like to think we're managing our lives well and nobody notices when something goes wrong. But in reality, those around us know we're not happy long before we do. By worrying too much about what others think of us, we end up striving rather than thriving. We set aside our dreams and ignore what's really troubling us because we can't deal with it.

We can't handle our feelings, so we jump into our car of life and start driving as fast as possible, so we can move away from the pain. "I can't stop," we tell ourselves. We know that if we *do* stop to look at the lies we've been telling ourselves (and often for long time), they will hit us hard. Little do we know that those lies have already taken over our lives.

Avoiding the truth

To avoid the truth we keep ourselves busy by taking on more work, going on more holidays and buying more stuff. We attend courses and fill our time with exercise classes. New diets, bigger cars and other forms of distraction protect us from the discomfort we feel with the fictitious and poisonous vision of the perfect, happy life. By keeping ourselves busy, we think we're spending our time doing what makes us happy, when in reality what we're doing is numbing and disconnecting ourselves from what matters and from a life that is true to who we are.

At some point we notice something is wrong, we get a bitter, uneasy feeling in our bodies. We start blaming the world for our misfortune. Then mental, emotional and physical exhaustion takes over as we're unable to deal with our feelings and we continue to look for answers outside of ourselves. Maybe you recognise some of the excuses you make for others and yourself when you're not dealing with your emotions or a particular situation.

- "Deep down he/she is a good person."
- "He/she is very stressed, this is why he/she reacts this way."
- "I need to work this hard to maintain this family."
- "This is what is expected of me."
- "I can't do it."
- "I don't qualify."

- "I don't have time."
- "I can't help it, I am weak."
- "She had bad experiences, and this is why she acts like this."

Do you recognise any of these excuses? If so, they probably feel like an easy way out, but they don't hide what you're avoiding or trying to escape.

I have been there and done it too; most of us have at one point or another in our lives. Denying the truth of a situation is like sitting on a rocking chair. It keeps us moving but it doesn't take us anywhere.

"The moment we lie to ourselves, we leave the moment."
Jeff Brown

As John approached his 50th birthday, he felt as if he was running on a hamster wheel; trapped, dissatisfied and bitter about his life. He had not been in love with his wife of 20 years for a long time. In his own words, "Nothing is wrong with her. We are simply the wrong match." According to him, his wife did not love him either.

To make matters worse, they work from home running their business together. There is not much sex in their relationship, almost no touching and no other form of affection. This makes them both feel unworthy, starved of love and emotionally numb. Of course, having this amount of tension in the house rubbed off on the children, impacting the development of their character and driving their behaviour.

In an attempt to sort things out, John sold the family home and bought a bigger house. He also bought a motorbike and started exercising, but nothing changed. In fact, things got even more complicated as he fell in love with another woman. He wouldn't get a divorce though, because he wanted to keep the family together.

This decision, far from sorting out the mess he'd made, left John feeling even more tense and miserable. He knew it was affecting his family. He was aware that his example was teaching his children that it's okay to treat others badly and lie to yourself about what you're doing.

One day, John armed himself with courage and, in the privacy of my kitchen, admitted to me what was wrong. He told me how this terrible situation was making him feel like a coward and a failure; he was disappointed with himself.

John's fear of change was so huge that he'd only make a change if he was forced to – either by his wife leaving him or by having a health scare. He kept telling himself he was behaving responsibly and sensibly by not breaking up his family. He couldn't admit that he was holding together a family that would be better off if it was apart.

John was still driving fast but going nowhere, blaming the world for his problems and accepting without question that this was his fate. He may never change, remaining a victim of his own choices and raising the victims of the future. Hopefully, he'll wake up in time to live his life and not the life others wished for him. He is the driver and the one who can change the direction or the destination at any time.

We can all be John. When we're stuck, we lose faith in our ability to change our lives. We become disconnected from what makes us feel alive so it's no wonder joy and balance disappear. There is always something we can do. We can change the story by being honest with ourselves. What makes the difference is the awareness and speed at which we're travelling in our journeys. By acknowledging and accepting the truth, pain diminishes and, ultimately, it's what we choose to do with the rest of the journey that changes the story.

Being honest with yourself is about more than pretending to have a perfect life. Being honest with yourself means facing your fears and acknowledging the discomfort that we hide by lying to ourselves. Instead, let's listen to the feedback we're getting from our bodies, thoughts and feelings and allow vulnerability and courage to take the lead. This is how we get closer to living a life that is true to ourselves. It's time for a new opportunity, time to dream again.

Explore the excuses you're making for yourself and see them for what they are: denial of the truth and avoidance of change. By accepting the truth and releasing the pain, we slow down and gain awareness of ourselves and our lives, freeing ourselves of our emotional paralysis and disconnection.

Time does not wait for anyone and before you know it, it's slipped away, along with your dreams. Change the story. Only then can you write a happy ending.

Empowering Actions

Answer the questions below for clarity:

- How would my life be affected if the people or situation that's making me unhappy were to disappear?
- Is what I'm holding onto essential for me to live a life of contentment?
- Is this who I am and is this what I've chosen or is it something I've allowed to develop in my mind until it has become my reality?
- What would I like to have happen next?

Running away from yourself is exhausting. You might think you can keep doing it and avoid changing what brought you to this point in the first place, but you can't. **Be honest with yourself.**

Maybe you're wondering what will happen if you carry on as you are? Some people will never admit anything is wrong. They'll just keep running forever and for as long as they can. They may barely be coping and have health problems, feel depressed, be irritable or even begin to rely on drugs and alcohol to mask their feelings of unease and discontentment. Others fall into a trap of victimhood, blaming the world for what is happening to them, forever bound up in chains of their own making. Yes, it takes courage to live the life we deserve. The good news is that you can free yourself at any time. Yes, you can! It's when you try to control everything and rush at life that you lose perspective because you disconnect from parts of yourself and from others along the way.

Spend some time alone to find the voice you have been suppressing for years. This is how you get to heal, create space and accept the discomfort.

Being honest with yourself might be scary, and yet it's what pushes you to take the next step. Just trust that you can handle it no matter what.

Do you have the strength to handle it? Yes, you do! It takes more energy to keep making excuses than it does to be honest. Letting go of the lies frees you from dullness and pain.

Think of something you know isn't quite right in your life. Imagine observing the situation from a distance. Take an objective look at it and see it for what it is, then accept it with no judgment. Allow any emotions to come up and notice how much easier and lighter you feel when you accept them. You can choose whether to make any changes or not, though just accepting and noticing how you feel will help. If you're ready, take some action because this is the only way to live a life that's congruent with your values and who you are.

Let's look into the future and imagine that you've seen what needs to change, accepted it and are taking action towards creating a better life. Showing up as your true self has attracted beautiful things into your life with ease. You have just changed the narrative.

This is real magic and you've created it. A decision is all it takes. Powerful, right?

To help you create your true life, you'll probably need some support, so talk to somebody you trust about how you feel and ask them to help you figure out what you're going to do. Talking helps you work things through so you can decide how you're going to achieve your objective. It's like drawing a road map; by sharing your decisions, you become accountable for them. By seeking support, you empower yourself to make the changes you want to make and little by little you learn to trust yourself and your ability to design your new life.

We often expect our partners or parents to give us the support we need, and when we don't get it, we think they've failed us. Remember though, those close to you aren't mind-readers. They don't know what you need unless you tell them. So, either ask for it or tell yourself the words of support you wish you could hear from your parents, teachers, friends, colleagues, husband or wife. What would you love them to tell you when you need their support?

Write down those words and start repeating them to yourself, rather than waiting to hear them from someone else. Never underestimate the power of words and what they can do for you. For me it was, "If they can, you can. Everything you desire is happening." Reciting this to myself has made a positive difference to my life. Explore what words might support you right now.

Set an intention to achieve something important to you; something that would alter what you believe and feel about yourself. Then create a mantra that supports you in achieving that outcome. Repeat it until you believe it and it becomes part of your thinking. When you've internalised that belief, create a new one and begin making that part of your thinking too.

Consider these beliefs:

- There is no failure, only learning and feedback.
- Life supports me.
- I trust myself.
- I can do it!
- There is a solution to every problem.

Which of these resonates with you? Find the right words for you and use them. It's very empowering. Just by telling yourself, "I can do it, no matter what!" will give you the confidence to do anything, to persevere and not give up, even when you feel scared and tired.

Beliefs such as these when repeated like a mantra with intention and attached to a desirable energy have helped my clients regain their power over their lives. They have accomplished things they never thought possible, only to discover that they can do and achieve as much as anyone else.

At one point, I fell asleep at the wheel of my own life and allowed someone else to jump into the driving seat. When my best friend ditched me and disappeared from my life because she didn't need me anymore, I felt paralysed emotionally. I was unhappy, irritable, and I felt misunderstood and unappreciated. But mostly I was angry with myself for giving away my power. When the pain became too much, I decided to go away for a few days. I needed time to listen to myself again.

Away from the distractions of my everyday life and family, I found the space to hear my soul speaking to me. I heard it tell me what I needed to address in my life. I had forgotten to connect with myself and do what made me feel alive. I understood on the first day away (and also the first moments of solitude I'd had in 10 years), that only by being honest with myself could I bring joy back into my life. I realised that I needed to change my perspective, take responsibility, make a choice and reclaim my power. My journey started by setting boundaries, revising my inner belief system and increasing the love and respect I felt for myself.

I thought of my dreams and what was essential to me to be happy and I decided to become my own best friend. I became playful with life again, allowing my inner child out in this playground called life. The results were phenomenal. In no time, I was able to laugh at myself again and take life as it comes, sometimes good, sometimes bad – and always trusting that whatever came my way I had the tools and resilience to handle it.

I reminded myself that life does not have to be perfect to be good. I became aware of my mortality and that I didn't know whether I was going to be here tomorrow. That's when the question came into my mind: "If not now, when?"

A thought started to come up every day: "Marina, if you were an endangered species, how would you take care of yourself? And guess what Marina, you *are* in danger of extinction, so you need to preserve, look after and nurture yourself; and one more thing Marina, you are resilient, enjoy life and let go of the future." Changing my perspective on life is all it took to shift everything for me. If anything in your life needs a change of direction, I encourage you look at it from a different vantage point. I know you can do this, because if I could do it, so can you. Today, I am happy and fully in charge of my life, taking responsibility for every bit of it: the high, the lows, everything! And it's that switch which has allowed me to live the way I choose.

Taking responsibility for your life means being brutally honest with yourself, so it's important to be kind to yourself by taking breaks and having fun. Stay aware of what's going on so you don't fall asleep at the wheel of your life and create a zone of honesty around yourself as far as possible. It's worth checking your thoughts with an imaginary metal detector in case there's a cheeky lie hiding and waiting to pounce at a later date. If you can't avoid the denial and can't face change for any reason, take responsibility for the choices you make.

Reflections

What legacy would you like to leave for your family and for humanity?

- I would love to leave…
- I would like my loved ones to remember me for…
- I would love to do/experience…

Ask yourself, how can you be in the world so you attract wonderful experiences into your life? Write down the answers and keep a record of them until you make them happen. Ditch anything or anyone who does not support you in being your best self, and remember that you're allowed to make mistakes – it's the way you learn and is a sign that you're actively engaging in life. Above all, don't take life too seriously. Reclaim your power by making decisions that support you to keep driving your amazing life. Take action, add passion, keep getting up when you fall and never settle for less than what you dream of having.

Live a life that's true to you. And of course, this is life, so it's unpredictable. Explore and embrace your perfectly imperfect life. Be patient. Knowing you can't control everything removes the drama from what happens around you. It opens a door for you to focus on what you can do and the way life can be when you embody the best version of yourself.

"There are bigger goals in life
than being a good person to others,
be a good person to yourself."

Unknown

Zesty Takeaways

- ♥ Life does not have to be perfect to be great.
- ♥ You have the resilience to live life's lows as well as the highs.
- ♥ Listen to what is hidden behind your excuses
- ♥ Set boundaries for yourself and others
- ♥ Reclaim your power and take what is essential with you
- ♥ Be your own best friend.
- ♥ **Aim high; you only have one life.**

Chapter 7

Owning Your Feelings

It's cold outside today, so when you arrive for your session, I bring a blanket to keep you warm so you feel comfortable and at home.

I make you lemon and ginger tea, hoping the refreshing flavours will balance the sweetness of the panettone I'm serving with it. I'm glad you're here to share it with me, otherwise I might have been tempted to eat it all myself!

You're telling me about what's been happening with you recently and, in the process, you share times when you've felt a range of uncomfortable emotions like sadness, anger and frustration.

"Let it hurt
Let it bleed
Let it heal
And then let it go."

Nikita Gill

Owning your feelings

If you're the kind of person who throws themselves into life and takes risks, it's important to remember that not everything will work out as you expect. Don't worry though, because rather than being a reason to stop, this is a sign to keep going because you're living.

Sometimes negative emotions are caused by something someone else has said or done. Other times it's because something has happened in our lives that has upset us. You can hit rock bottom for any number of reasons. When that happens, you may experience anxiety, lack of motivation, anger and sadness.

"What shall we do with all these emotions? I feel as if I'm drowning in them," you say.

"You let them go," I reply.

Let it go

When we talk about happiness, joy and self-love we refer to these emotions as positive. On the other hand, fear, pain and loneliness are associated with something negative. The truth is that all of these feeling are just different emotions.

We are willing to express joy but avoid feeling pain or even running the risk of feeling pain. Avoiding pain consumes us and causes us a considerable number of problems, from emotional numbness and health complaints to psychological issues. Being open to all of your emotions is part of being open to love. It allows you mental freedom as well as the possibility of many of the other wonderful experiences life has to offer.

Nobody wants to feel negative emotions for any longer than necessary and the best way to deal with those feelings is to move through them by allowing them space to be expressed.

Remember that your story and experiences are important, and I encourage you to take your time and share your experiences with someone supportive who can hold a safe space for you. There's nothing better than a good chat with a friend, though if you want professional help, you can see a counsellor, therapist or coach.

The more you talk about what happened, the more you'll learn about yourself and what went on, which means its power over you will diminish. Take care, though, not to get stuck in the past or get too wound into one event. By understanding how your mind and body respond to particular incidents, the more you'll learn about how to heal and let go.

Move gently through the highs and lows of life and you'll quickly restore balance and your energy. You'll discover the mighty power of resilience and that you have the emotional tools to cope with anything that happens. **Whichever way you choose to deal with it, accept what is happening, allow some transition time and then let go.**

Cry it out

When you're sad, cry until you have no more tears. Don't hold back. And when you're done crying, let all the emotions go. In the olden times (as my kids say – they think I'm prehistoric) and when I was much younger, we were told not to cry. How crazy! Crying is the body's best release mechanism. It's comforting to cry and tears help us express our sadness, pain and frustration.

A few weeks ago, the toilet in my bathroom leaked. I placed a bucket under the drip and forgot about it. Before I knew it, the bucket had overflowed and there was water everywhere. It taught me a lesson: empty the bucket before the water overflows otherwise there'll be an even bigger mess. It's the same with crying. If you stop yourself from crying, your emotions will overflow elsewhere. It could result in you breaking down completely, being ill or hurting others. There is no more to it – if you're full of emotion, empty it out.

However, it's not always as simple as it sounds and many people struggle to express their emotions by crying. If you find it hard to cry, look for other ways of letting go (without hurting anyone, of course). Letting the anger out at the right time and place is a good practice and a safe one too.

Repressed anger

Life presents us with a whole heap of restrictions, rules and deadlines as well as people we find challenging to deal with. When in pain, we often become aware of the negative effect it has on us and it's only normal to feel angry and frustrated. Although anger and frustration are unpleasant emotions, they are also a sign that we care and more importantly, that we're alive.

When I was little, a lady called Encarna would help my mum with the household chores. One day, she was cooking a lentil stew using the pressure cooker. She'd added all the ingredients, closed the lid and put the pan on the stove. For a while, the whole house smelt delicious, until... *boom!!!*

When we went into the kitchen, we saw the lid of the pressure cooker stuck to the ceiling and lentils scattered everywhere. They looked like polka dots on a white dress. Encarna had accidentally blocked the pressure release valve, so when the pressure built and couldn't be released, the pan exploded hurling the lid and the contents everywhere. I thought it was very funny (I still do), until I remembered that we'd have to call my mum at work and tell her the news. Encarna and I knew that wasn't going to be as funny as the explosion.

This is how anger works too, which is why it's essential to let it out before it leads to more destructive consequences, like lashing out at people or becoming aggressive or moody. Not only can you not sort out anything when you're in an uncontrollable rage, it'll also make you feel bitter, leaving you with physical pain. Taken to the extreme, some of this pain can change into auto-immune illnesses, chronic illness or depression, which diminishes the quality of your life. So, let off steam now and then, rather than blowing a gasket!

Dealing with anger

A friend once taught me a valuable method of releasing emotions that never fails to deliver. She worked in a gift shop selling small and inexpensive decorative ornaments. She never understood why some customers were so demanding when their investment was so small. When a customer hit a nerve with their unrealistic demands, rather than getting angry with them, she would excuse herself saying she had to go to the stock room. There she had a massive green rubbish bin and a hammer. She used to hit the corner of the lid with the hammer repeatedly until she'd let out all her frustration.

By the time she came out of the stock room and into the shop to deal with her customer again, she had a massive smile on her face and was able to give them great service. It only took a minute and it meant she didn't have to make excuses or get angry with anyone – it was just the rubbish bin that suffered! It's a powerful technique and best of all, it doesn't cost anything! It simply allows you to release your emotions without hurting yourself or anyone else.

So far, you have gained some clarity and have dealt with your emotions. Now it's time to take responsibility. Which beliefs need changing? After all, you don't want to go through the same reactions again or these feelings will become part of your identity. What feedback are you getting about yourself from this experience? What's the learning in this? Be as honest with yourself as you possibly can. How does knowing all this and putting a few changes in place alter your potential future experiences?

Empowering Actions

Follow these strategies so you can get the help and support you need. Use the one you like best but try to explore them all at some point.

Step 1

When you're feeling angry or frustrated, write down what triggered those emotions. Write to the person who upset you and tell them how you feel and why. You can swear if you feel like. It feels good to let it out. Wait a few days then look back at what you wrote. Read about what happened as if you're learning about it for the first time. This will help you make sense of the emotions so you can experience the event from another perspective. When you've done that and had a chance to process your feelings, burn, bin or tear up what you wrote if you want to.

Step 2

Be your own best friend. What advice would you give to a friend who'd experienced the same emotions as you? How would you support him or her? We're usually very good at supporting others, but rarely give ourselves the same level of support.

Step 3

Ask yourself:

- Who will I talk to so I can share these feelings?
- What is it like to be in this place emotionally?
- Where would I like to be emotionally instead?
- How can I move on from this event?
- What am I going to do, and when?
- How am I going to stick to a plan so I don't go back to feeling that way?

Step 4

Find a healthy way of releasing your frustration. Think about what your own version of the hammer and bin might be. When you know what it is, do it until you don't have any more frustration left inside you.

Step 5

If you don't already do it, build exercise into your day. It doesn't matter what you do, as long as you enjoy it. Try boxing, walking and yoga. For your mental health, try meditation, reiki healing, talking to others, painting or anything else you want to try out or that you enjoy.

Find out what works for you. It's easy to dismiss possible solutions based on previous experience. Avoid this if you can – you've changed and your life is changing, so what didn't work before, might work now.

With your new-found awareness, you might discover something you weren't giving yourself or didn't know you needed. Allow yourself to have it. Give yourself permission to have love, fun, attention, success, time, praise, support and anything else you want. Take charge of your story by driving your life forward using your emotions as a guide.

It is not what happens to you, it is what you do with what happens to you that matters.

Look around at what you have – nature, friends, family, your body and mind – and express gratitude. If there was a negative event in your life, it's behind you; it's part of your story but not your whole story. Acknowledge how this event has made you who you are today: stronger, wiser and more resilient. **Trust yourself because trust grows love, and love expands your life.**

"Your life is like a balloon... if you never
Let yourself go, you will never
Know how far you can rise."

Linda Poindexter

Zesty Takeaways

- ♥ Acceptance is the first step to moving on from painful emotions.
- ♥ Allow yourself to explore all your emotions, not just the acceptable ones.
- ♥ Give yourself time to process your feelings then take action when you're ready.
- ♥ Let the pressure out before you explode and your emotions cause damage.
- ♥ Tell your story, it's important.
- ♥ **Trust yourself. Trust grows love and love expands your life.**

Chapter 8

The Power of Choice

You arrive early today, excited about our session. As I make the coffee, I explain what I want us to talk about next. "We have talked about many significant subjects so far," I say. "Today we are exploring who you are and who you want to be. You see, you have choices and we're going to explore the ways in which you can make those choices and do so in a way that supports you in being the person you want to be.

"Who are you? What defines you? What is important to you? What do you want from life? These are all huge questions, and I know you might not know the answer to them. That's fine, because we're going to look for the answers together."

Knowledge is power

Imagine you're driving on a dark, foggy night. There's almost no visibility and you feel disorientated and unsure about where you're going. What are you going to do? Is it a good idea to continue driving when you don't know where you are? Or are you going to stop and wait until it gets light and the fog has cleared?

"In order to clean the house
You need to see the dirt first."

Louise Hay

Let's explore the metaphor about driving in the fog. Knowing what you want helps you make choices with more ease. If you don't know what you want, it's okay. You're simply at the start of your journey and need to decide where you want to go. On the other hand, if you're already on the road but you're not sure where you're going, you'll feel confused and vulnerable. Ultimately, you won't get very far and you'll have to stop at some point to work out where you want to get to.

Knowing who you are gives you confidence, a sense of direction and a feeling of inner power. It raises your self-esteem. I dare to say, knowing who you are and what are you willing to do (or not) is more important than choosing which house you are going to live in.

Knowing what you want gives you drive and makes you more productive. When you know what you want, the fears and doubts take up less space. They might not go away completely, but they won't take up such a big space in your life because they never have the chance to develop. Action is an antidote to fear and the more you achieve, the more motivated you become as you can see your dreams materialise before your eyes. Soon, success becomes your new normal.

We all want to have a great life and be happy. If you've been happy before, what was it like? If you've been unhappy, what was that like? If you've never been happy, how will you know when you've achieved it? Replace doubts with clarity by knowing yourself and what you want.

When you know what you want, it's like having a blindfold removed. Without that clarity of vision, you won't know the difference between what you have and what you want. You can't tell whether you're unhappy or just hungry or tired and whether you love someone or just feel comfortable with them. Lack of clarity robs you of choice because if you don't know what you want, you can't make a choice at all.

What kind of life would you live if you could have any kind of life at all? Explore this question then write what comes to mind and explain why it matters to you. What would that life allow you to be, do or have that you can't currently be, do or have? How would you feel if you did have that life? It might take a while to figure out what it is you want and that's okay. Keep thinking and writing until you get a feeling in your body that the life you're describing is right for you.

You might find that what you want is more excitement, love or fulfilment. When you've identified that missing part, you can begin to build it into your life.

Forgiving the past

We are now going to look at the lives of two amazing women who discovered who they wanted to be after a key event in their life.

Choose what is good for you!

Anna was a woman who worked hard to care for her family and held down a job as part of her husband's business. She did this almost completely on her own as her husband was often away and unable to help her with family commitments.

One day, I asked her what she would have chosen to do as a job if she hadn't worked as part of her husband's business. She told me, she would have been a chef, but hadn't been aware that this avenue was open to her.

"Nobody ever helped me explore what I wanted or the options available to me. I didn't know I could have a purpose. I was never praised for anything I did well and I didn't know what my values were or what I liked or didn't like. As a result, I spent half my life asleep at the wheel. I had no directions and no map to follow. I had no confidence and didn't value myself. I didn't know what I wanted," she told me.

"Now I know that I had a lot of potential and had many choices. I could have taken an easier path in life, but I had no sense of direction for my life. I discovered all this late in life, after I'd been looking for a place to belong but never found it.

"Now I know that nobody else can give me a sense of purpose and that it is my responsibility to find it for myself. Today, I'm in charge and I make sure my family and friends know they have the power to choose what is right for them.

"I have no regrets; I have made peace with my story. I live fully, and in the present, making sure I don't fall asleep at the wheel of my life again. I take great delight in seeing my children choosing what they want to do and be, and that heals me. It helps me rewrite my own story and ensures that what happened to me doesn't happen to them.

"It's never too late to live life on your own terms. I've learned that self-forgiveness is the way forward as it helps me heal, learn, accept and move on."

Anna's story shows how not knowing what we want can change the course of our lives forever. Her life could have been very different if she'd known who she wanted to be. Yet she showed me beautifully how peace sets us free to write a fresh story or pick up an old story where we left it. It isn't about what happened in the past, it's about what can happen when we learn to leave the past behind. Choosing to change perspective and learn creates opportunities and empowers future generations to do better. Anna's story proves it's never too late to live life on our own terms.

Clarity and making conscious choices can steer our lives in a new direction; but sometimes it's not enough. How can a person who hasn't been given the chance to choose the life they want when young feel free to choose what they want at a later date?

Let me introduce you to Melissa; she was born in Santo Domingo and lives in Spain. Melissa's mother left Spain to look for better opportunities and they lost contact. It took them a long time to reconcile and reunite with each other. By the time Melissa got in touch with me, she'd had enough of her own chronic negativity and was tired of listening to her own excuses

I asked her: "Regardless of your past, who do you want to be?" At that moment something changed. She suddenly saw that she could choose who she wanted to be, not just live with the set of events, experiences and circumstances that had shaped her life until now. Finally, she felt free. She accepted her past for what it was, including the lows. She saw that she was not alone because she had herself to rely on. She even got a tattoo that read: *Optimism is a must if I want to live to the max.*

I asked her the following questions so she could explore further. Use them to gain clarity around your own choices.

Explore the following questions:

What do you do that lights a fire in your heart and makes you happy?

Is there something you do that totally engrosses you? Something where hours pass without you noticing. It's that thing you talk about incessantly when you're with friends and family. That thing you talk about until everyone is sick of hearing about, it is your passion and it deserves to be explored.

What do you see yourself doing in the future?

Look at your life afresh and look for opportunities to use your best and most enjoyable skills. Be curious and enrol in courses. Study, learn and read everything you can about what interests you. The fact that you are methodical and well-organised doesn't mean you have to be someone's PA. What about starting a decluttering business or training as an accountant?

For example, you might be passionate about basketball and know everything there is to know about it. But that doesn't mean you're going to become a professional basketball player (you might be too old or not have the physique to succeed). Yet even though you might not be able to be a basketball player, you can still be a basketball coach or a basketball journalist. What could be better than spending all day talking about what you love?

Allow others to support you in finding out about aspects of yourself you may not be aware of. Ask friends or family what they think your biggest strengths are then write down the answers in your journal or a notebook. You'll be surprised by some of the answers and insights you get from others.

When you have an idea about what you want to do, ask yourself if this is something you'd still like to do for more than three, five or 10 years. If the answer is "No", then this is not the work you were born for.

Be your wild, raw and authentic self. And don't play small – it won't get you anywhere. Listen to your gut and ditch playing the role of the person others want you to be. Encourage yourself – it's amazing how a few words of encouragement can move you forward quickly.

One more thing – dare to dream, explore your ideas and declutter your life. This is what Melissa did. Through self-exploration, Melissa discovered her passion and what she was brilliant at. By sharing her inspirational quotes through printing them on clothes, she created the foundations for her new business. Today, she publishes stories and poems and reads them aloud on radio. She also has an extra job that pays for the production of her merchandise and allows her to sell it anywhere in the world. Her products have Melissa's essence in them and embody her decision to choose the life she wants for herself.

Her story proves that you can change at any time – as long as you have the determination and readiness to fight for yourself. At the very least, you can choose how to feel, which means you're freer than you might think you are.

No clarity = vague destination
Vague destination = difficult journey

Identifying your essentials

Let's explore what is essential for you and how you can ensure you build those essentials into your life when making a decision. Essentials are the elements of your life that are important and have meaning for you. Your values are the source of your foundations – they will always be with you no matter how long or short the journey you're on. They represent the factors you're not ready to compromise on.

Roy Disney said: "It is not hard to make decisions when you know what your values are." This is because when you know what matters to you, it's easy to make choices. If you don't value something, you won't choose it. Think about a simple career choice. If you value your independence, you probably won't decide to do a job involving shift work or that requires you to work away from home for long periods. You're far more likely to be attracted by having your own business or working as a contractor because both offer you autonomy and independence.

What matters to you? Is it financial security? Creativity? Doing meaningful work? Though it doesn't have to be work-related, of course. Your values can influence where you choose to live or the way you take care of yourself.

Consider what attributes someone needs for you to want to share your life with them? I'm not talking about money or superficial things like how they look, but their principles and values. What is essential to you and what couldn't you live without? Write it down.

A key essential for me is loyalty and generosity. I didn't want to live with someone who I couldn't trust or who was mean with money. My husband is loyal and loves his family. And he's generous

– if I ask him to buy me half a dozen eggs, he'll probably bring me at least another dozen. He'd bring me the hen if he had the chance!

Looking back, I now realise that if I'd had more clarity about what I wanted, I could have asked for more. That wasn't something I learned to do until much later in life.

Making decisions is easier when you know what you value.

The Non-Negotiables

I knew what my essentials were, but I didn't know what was non-negotiable in my life or that it was my responsibility to choose what I wanted. Non-negotiables are those things you are not prepared to negotiate over under any circumstances. It's about setting boundaries. Boundaries show others where you stand and help to raise your self-esteem by making it easier to put yourself (or what is important to you) first. They clearly communicate what you are and are not prepared to do as well as helping you stay organised.

When you don't have boundaries in place, your life can get crazy. One client of mine had nine meetings every day. Others read their emails in bed, others worked so much they couldn't get to the loo and some skipped lunch because they were too busy to eat. All of these overworked people allowed this to happen because they hadn't set any boundaries and didn't know what a non-negotiable looked like for them.

Fortunately, today things are different for these clients: they limit meetings, make time for lunch (and the loo) and no longer read work emails in bed. As a result, their lives have improved substantially. All of them reported to me that once they'd set boundaries, their life became easier and they were less stressed. At last they felt as if they had control of their lives, rather than the other way around.

Any time you set boundaries based on your non-negotiables, you take a risk. If you decide that starting work before 9am is a non-negotiable, you have to accept that you might lose clients who want meetings earlier in the morning. That's a good thing though, because you won't feel compromised or pressurised to do anything you don't want to do. Of course, you can change your non-negotiables any time so they always fit with your current lifestyle and needs.

Empowering Action

Write a list of your essentials and non-negotiables. This will give you a clear picture of how you want your life to be. It'll also help you set boundaries that will simplify your life and ensure others respect your time and priorities.

If you only take one thing from this chapter, know this: clarity about what you want and the decision to make it happen are the essential tools for living the life **you desire**. Without those two elements in place, your journey becomes unnecessarily difficult. When you remember that it's YOUR CHOICE, you can take responsibility for yourself and your life.

Knowing what you are good at and what is essential in your life allows you to make choices that give your life direction, making the journey easier and more straightforward. Knowledge gives you power, inner knowledge sets you on fire. As the fog in your brain lifts, you begin to explore what is behind your initial thoughts with greater clarity, becoming aware of your choices.

"Don't ask me what the world needs.
Ask me what makes you come alive,
go and do it because what the world needs
are people who have come alive."

Howard Thurman

Zesty Takeaways

- Clarity = destination = easier journey = better results
- Knowledge gives you power, inner knowledge sets you on fire.
- Non-negotiable + essentials = clarity and power
- Your choices, your outcomes. Choose wisely.
- **Make sure what you choose makes you happy.**

Chapter 9

Everyone's Got an Ego

It's a gorgeous sunny day outside. The spring is here, gifting us an explosion of colour everywhere. We decide to sit in the garden this time. I always find that the places we meet and what we drink or eat influences how the conversation flows, the way we approach things and how we process information. Our environment matters more than we think.

You start by telling me that you argued with your dad because he always thinks he's right. What's worse, despite you being middle-aged, he still treats you like a child, dismissing what you are saying. He always thinks you're wrong and he's right.

Who knows best?

How many times have you heard this before: I'm right, you're wrong? You've even heard people you barely know – as well as family and friends – say this. It seems as if we're surrounded by experts who are all far too willing to give us their unsolicited feedback and teach us freely that they are right and of course, we are wrong. Maybe you've even been one of those experts because we all think we're right and someone else is wrong at some point in our life.

When we're told by someone else that we're wrong, our ego is hurt. We get angry and feel inadequate, as if we're not enough. It's as if someone has taken away a piece of us. Our ego gets angry and demands justice, wanting the piece back that has been taken.

Let's make one thing clear: we all have egos. It's part of being human and we can't just get rid of it. And, to a certain extent, we wouldn't want to because our egos can be of help, for example, when we need motivation. It's when our ego takes control that we lose the ability to appreciate others for who they are and life for what it is.

Constantly trying to prove ourselves and influence what others think means we'll never be able to live in the present. Our life will be full of anxiety and fear, disconnecting us from others. Those who always think they're right and know better tend to be very controlling. Anyone who wants to have control over others is rarely happy, as they find it difficult to trust life, other people or their environment, meaning they can never relax.

"Most people do not listen with the intent to understand; they listen with the intent to reply."

Stephen Covey

You can't truly listen to anyone else when you think you know better. When you tell someone else they're wrong and that you know best, what you're really saying is that you're better than them. Park your ego and you're guaranteed learning.

The difference between someone with an inflated ego and someone who believes in their viewpoint is that the self-assured person doesn't need to win, nor do they need recognition that they're right from others.

Resisting your ego

Let's explore our egos and what we can do to turn things around. Think for a minute about the type of people who take pleasure in telling you you're wrong, that this is not how it is done, and this way is better. When you look at them and their lives, ask yourself, are they happy, connected, sensitive people who love to cooperate and help others? Or are they dogmatic and stuck in their thinking and behaviour? Perhaps they feel insecure and scared.

One day, when I was in my early twenties and still living in Spain, I was having breakfast in a coffee shop opposite a church because I had some time to waste. I don't know what prompted me but before I knew it, I was inside the church and sitting in the confession booth. This was surprising because although I was raised as a Catholic, I hadn't been in a church since I was confirmed, apart from a few weddings. Despite this, God and I are good friends. We argue a lot about why bad things happen to good people, and we speak daily as I always have something to say, so we have a good connection. When the priest asked me to tell him my sins, I didn't have much to say. I went through the list of all the capital sins and commandments and I hadn't transgressed in any area except for not going to church for a long time. Yet I didn't consider this a sin.

The priest told me, "You are wrong, you are very wrong. It is a sin not to come to the house of God to pray." I, of course, without hesitation unleashed the passionate dragon within and ended up having a heated discussion with him. I explained my views on God to him, that he is everywhere and in me. And about how it wasn't necessary for me to go to church for a chat; I had my own private line to God. I told him I regretted coming to confession at all.

He was trying to convince me of my 'wrongdoing' and make me believe he was doing me a favour for absolving me. "No need to absolve me," I replied. "With that attitude, you won't go very far. God is love and you are the antithesis of love." Not content with that pronouncement, I continued, "You need to prove to people that what they are doing is wrong. That need is so big, it has taken you away from your initial goal and is preventing you from doing your job." And feeling very high and mighty, I left.

I could almost taste his ego – but I could also taste mine. I was upset that he'd told me what was best for me. Yet, I'd never planned to argue with him, so I had a chat with myself about what I'd done. I realised that rather than exploring why going to church was important for him, I had sunk to his level showing no empathy or control, I'd behaved as badly as him. What I'd just witnessed and been the artifice of an ego-to-ego fight, with each of us trying to prove the other wrong. How sad.

When we indulge in this sort of behaviour, it's like trying to drive our car with a massive weight attached to it making it impossible to get up any speed. Everything is slow, so you need more fuel to go a shorter distance, the engine strains and doesn't drive smoothly. All in all, it's not a happy car.

If that were to happen today, I would put myself in that priest's shoes and look at what going to church regularly meant for him. Then I would put myself in the shoes of someone who is observing the scene and I would give myself better advice on how to handle the situation. I would reply with compassion, respect and love.

It's with love that we build bridges of acceptance and respect. Everyone feels heard and there's no need to show you are right and someone else is wrong. Think about how you can respect and value others by putting yourself in their shoes. Understand what brought them to that way of thinking and advise yourself to sort out the situation with kindness, not anger.

Empowering Actions

Write a list of all the people you know who are dominated by their need to be right (we all know someone like this). Once you have identified them, think about their lives and how they live.

- How happy do you think they are?
- What do these people have in common?
- What do you think it's like to be like them?
- Would you like to be like them?
- Do you like to be on the receiving end of their behaviour?

If you want to be happy, drop the need to be right. Quieten your ego and keep your energy for the moments when you really need to be heard. Every time you feel the urge to tell someone they're wrong, answer these questions and say whether this argument brings you peace, connects you to the other person or divides you. Put yourself in their shoes and understand that **what they're saying is true for them, even if it's not true for you**. Look for a solution and keep your ego in line, otherwise you'll hurt yourself as well as them before you've realised winning the argument wasn't worth it.

Step 1

Remember a time when you were fiercely trying to prove that you were right about something. Hold that vision for a while.

- Did it make either of you into better people?
- Did either of you learn anything from your disagreement?
- Did both parties feel supported?

Step 2

Now think about that moment again, only this time, imagine you are an outsider watching the argument. How does watching it from a distance help you see it differently?

- Knowing what you now know, explore how can you change the story to make it positive and free yourself from the need to prove others wrong.
- Consider how you would react to the same situation now, and how you would get your message across differently.
- Apply all the above when you find yourself in a similar situation.

I'm not saying you shouldn't engage in challenging conversations, far from it. I'm feisty and I would never stay quiet about anything that mattered to me. What I am saying though, is that when you focus on yourself, you disengage from the world. Stand up, make sure that what matters, matters, but choose carefully when and how you do it. Sometimes you have to think about the long-term gain and not short-term satisfaction.

When you love your life more than you love your ego, life becomes more enjoyable.

Zesty Takeaways

- If it doesn't make you a better person, drop it.
- Put yourself in their shoes
- Love your life more than your ego: that's a sound way to enjoy your life.
- **The fundamental reason you are here is to live the best possible life.**

Chapter 10

Limiting Beliefs

We have been gifted another beautiful spring day. Living in the UK, we know not to take it for granted as it could be raining in a few days, so we decide to sit in the garden again. I ask you what your week has been like.

"Well, my scented candle company is thriving and we just had our biggest week since I started the business – I've even had to employ more staff. I've decided it's time to step up and start selling to wholesalers. I have everything I need to make this step up, but there's something stopping me; a fear that stems from something I heard when I was a child. It sounds ridiculous because it was such a long time ago, and yet every time I make progress towards my goals and create something awesome, it takes me back to that moment. I remember it so well. Someone told me nobody was going to ever buy my work and I would never achieve anything in life".

"Magic is believing in yourself,
If you can do that,
You can make anything happen."
Johann Wolfgang von Goethe

The fact that you remember this event tells me that it's in your conscious mind, which is why you're aware of it. Had it been a subconscious memory, you wouldn't be able to recall it. This is good news because when a limiting belief is out there for us to see, we can't unsee it, and that makes it easier to change. You can't allow a limiting belief to rule you. It could restrict your vision, your life and even your business or career. Fortunately, you can change that belief using specific techniques. As Socrates said, "The secret of change is to focus all your energy, not on fighting the old, but on building the new."

Shoulda, woulda, coulda

Your beliefs can either help you conquer the world or ruin your life, they're that powerful! I experienced this first hand when I went to London with a group of friends one weekend. While we were out, we met Erick. He introduced himself and told us he was a painter and decorator.

A few minutes into the conversation, it became clear to us that he was smart, funny and quick-witted. He had us all laughing with his hilarious banter and repartee. His talent was so clear that my friend asked him if he'd ever considered changing careers to be a stand-up comedian.

"Who me?" he replied. He stopped for a moment and his face changed. "Well, that was what I always wanted to do, but I couldn't do it because I am not very smart. If I could have done it, I would have..." He went quiet. Then he went on, "I come from a poor working-class family and my mum says people like us never do anything worth mentioning."

It was shocking to hear him say that, yet like many others, he was stuck with a belief that had literally stopped him in his tracks. Worse still, it had been planted at a very early age. He could have changed that belief and the course of his life, but he had no idea he could do that. He just accepted it as fact and lived accordingly. He was a man with a bag full of dreams who couldn't change the direction his life had taken because of a belief that he'd never amount to anything.

Fortunately, it's not always like this and that conversation reminded me of my brother's story. At the age of 11, Javier Levòn dreamed of being a fashion designer. He read all the fashion magazines our mother bought and sketched his own ideas of what beauty meant for him. When he mentioned to our mother that he wanted to be a fashion designer, he was quickly silenced. It wasn't a typical career for a man at that time, and certainly not in our town. The situation in the family and the social conditions made it impossible for him to become a fashion designer, or so he thought.

From that day onwards, he filled his time as much as he could – all in a bid to distract himself from the voice inside that was calling him to fulfil his purpose. He did lots of jobs and tried many different careers, but none of them satisfied him. Even if they started well, he simply didn't have the drive, passion or excitement to make them work.

After the novelty of each new job wore out, he was left feeling empty and lacking in direction. Many years later, he finally decided it was time to follow his dreams. At last, he was ready to challenge the social norms and his environment, and accept that he had a gift to share with the world, which instantly gave meaning to his life. He thought about what made him happier than anything else and it was designing clothes, so he replaced his old belief with a new one: that he was born to be a designer. From that moment on, his life changed.

When I asked him why it had taken him so long, he told me: "Dreams grow and evolve. Even when we know who we are and what we want, it takes time to accept the challenges that come with following our path. It took belief, self-love, patience and acceptance to realise my normal might not be the same as other people's normal. Now I know that loving what you do and living your life's purpose is the definition of success! When you add family and friends to that you have a recipe for happiness. I feel I have already succeeded because I have learned to believe in myself and trust my inner voice. Even when at times I can't hear it, I have faith and the clarity to follow myself and not the world. I now understand what it means to drive one's life and live a life true to oneself."

To fast-forward, today Javier Levòn brings beauty to what he describes as the force that moves the world around: women. By arranging fashion shows and designing dresses for women from all corners of the world he is doing what he does best. He is a great example of someone who changed his destiny and made his dreams come true.

The difference between these two men is that one was limited by his beliefs and the other wasn't. It might have taken time, but Javier changed his thinking and, with that, who he wanted to be.

"All it takes is one person in
any generation to heal a
family's limiting beliefs."

Gregg Braden

That's why I know you can achieve anything too. Though, as you already know, following a dream is not comfortable, you are required to step out of your comfort zone every single day. And you know what? It's worth it and means you won't get to the end of your life saying, "I wish I'd done something different".

Empowering Actions

Reflect on your life and write the answers to the following questions.

- What are your dreams?
- What are your fears about fulfilling those dreams?
- What happened in your life to stop you from being who you wanted to be?
- Is that true today?
- How far back does that belief go?
- Who made you believe it?
- Who would you be if you didn't have that belief?

Believe in yourself

Remember, it's not the situation you're in that prevents you from being who you want to be, it's your belief about your situation. Dreams do come true if you believe in yourself. The good news is that you can change your path any time you want to. How?

First, accept that you are in control of your life and that it is your responsibility to make it the life you want it to be.

Check your beliefs frequently to make sure they're not limiting you. If you discover a belief that is holding you back, change it. Think beyond your genes, environment and behaviours; challenge them and create the belief that you can achieve your goals. Remember you have all the resources you need to succeed, and you'll find them when you're willing to access them.

Look at it this way... you're on a road trip and have a destination in your sights. The hotels are booked, your route is planned and you're all set up for a wonderful trip. However, as you drive, you realise that you hate the road you're driving on, and the scenery and weather are awful. You decide to change direction and take a different route. Now, you're going somewhere different and, even though you know your journey might be longer for a while, it'll be worth it when you arrive. It takes effort to make the decision but as long as it is you who is driving, you lead the way.

Your passengers may or may not like the change in destination. You might even lose some of them on the way. And if they love you, they'll support you and be flexible enough to understand that what you're doing is best for everyone.

Let me introduce you to James, a successful entrepreneur and someone I admire greatly. He was a terrible student and finished school with just a single qualification in Home Economics. His tutor told him he'd be very lucky to get even an unskilled job.

At the time, James had no focus in his life. It was after hitting rock bottom and spending some time thinking things through that something changed. He found himself a job and soon after founded a charity aimed at giving better opportunities to talented but disadvantaged children in his area.

What changed?

He replaced his fears and limited vision of the world for dreams. He broke free from the stories he and others told him and committed to creating something bigger than himself. He changed his beliefs and with that his destiny.

The difference between someone who achieves their goals and someone who doesn't is perseverance and faith. The person who never gives up – and has an unbreakable faith even when things get difficult – is the one who reaches their destination.

James' path isn't easy. He suffers from Crohn's disease and arthritis. Sometimes, those health conditions get the better of him but they haven't stopped him from achieving another one of his dreams: swimming the English Channel. He had to put in a huge amount of effort to make this happen because of his health challenges, but he did it. Today, he is a successful business owner, with a wonderful lifestyle and a fulfilling role as someone who helps others do better.

If I told you that he wrote a book and competed in many triathlons and iron man competitions (amongst other things), you might think he's a superhero. He's not. He's simply a man with many dreams who **decided** to build beliefs that supported who he wanted to be.

Empowering Actions

Step 1

Think back to a time when someone told you that you were bad at something.

Step 2

Next, ask yourself whether you still believe it.

Step 3

Does it fit with the person you want to be? And if it doesn't, how can you change it? Remember, you can do anything you choose if you want to and if you're willing to put in the time and effort. See the possibilities and then commit yourself to making it happen. Share your dreams with someone who can hold you accountable and ask for help when you need it.

Step 4

Imagine you could accomplish your dreams and say "If I could, I would..." and state something you could do to achieve your goals. Continue like this until you can't think of anything else you can do. Then connect with the emotion of accomplishing these dreams. And don't let anyone tell you anything different.

Step 5

Imagine a ladder in front of you, each step being what you need to do in order to achieve your goals. How do you eat an elephant? Bit by bit. Take one small step that you believe you can make happen if you put in the effort. When you've accomplished it, choose another and then another. Before you know it, you'll reach the last step.

Step 6

Create a plan as to how you're going to make it happen. Ask yourself:

- What is my first step?
- When could I start implementing it?
- Who could support me and hold me accountable?
- What is at risk, and is my goal worth that risk?

Step 7

Replace any limiting beliefs that could hold you back with a belief that empowers you and encourages you to move forward. Notice what happens as you explore this thought. Each day, reset the intention to achieve your dream, attach it to an elevated emotion and how the result is going to make you feel.

There will be days when the road is tough. That's when it's time to transform challenges into fuel and not let the bad days win. Have faith in what you are setting out to do. We all have doubts when we strive for something that matters to us, and that's okay. If it's important to you, you will stay invested, if not you will make an excuse. **Remind yourself of how your heart is set alight when you think about who you can be.**

Look at where you are now and where you want to be and then allow your mind to access your inner child – the part of you that once dreamed you could do it. Give yourself permission to explore it and allow the seed to grow. As you start working towards making your dream a reality, it might feel strange. Explore whatever happens with the eyes of a curious child and say to yourself, "oh, that's interesting!" and just keep going.

Give yourself permission to dream and be curious. You can make magic happen.

Zesty Takeaways

- It is never too late to live the life you wanted to live
- If you don't accept that this is true, build a new belief and make magic happen.
- Replace fears for dreams – and empowerment!
- Find your strengths and ask for help.
- Challenges are part of life, transform them into fuel for your journey.
- **Only you can choose how your journey will end!**

PART TWO

ENJOY THE RIDE

Your power has emerged, you are ready for something new. All the strategies you've learned so far can take you a long way to achieving the life you want, but they can't guarantee happiness.

This part of the book is all about connecting with others, celebrating life and finding your zest. When you combine this with the first part of the book, you create balance and harmony in your life.

Most of us dream of living our life to the full, yet most of us struggle to achieve it. Conditioned by society and the demands of adulthood we tend to settle for less than we dreamed of having, probably only remembering to 'live' at weekends or when we're on holiday.

Positivity, sense of humour, fun and joy are the pillars of a zesty life. It's what makes us excited and what connects us with ourselves and others so we can enjoy the ride.

Apply the principles of fun, enjoyment and connection as you want to experience them in your daily life. **Whatever makes you feel excited and feeds your soul will generate joy in your life.**

One more piece of advice… keep it simple!

"Life should
Not only be lived,
It should
Be celebrated."

Osho

Chapter 11

Living in the Moment

You have changed so much since your first visit to my kitchen that I can see it in the way you stand. You look taller and straighter. Your presence is calmer and you talk about yourself with respect. You're clear on the non-negotiables in your life, who sets the rules and where you are going.

I cut watermelon and bring out some berries, neither of us fancies coffee or tea, so we have some juice. You're sharing with me that you are about to start your summer holiday and explaining that you've decided to stop feeling guilty when you're not constantly busy. You're ready to live in the moment and would love a few tips on how to do just that.

I agree. Even the simplest pleasures like eating, drinking, taking time off or napping can make us feel as though we're being lazy or over-indulgent. We can so easily end up feeling guilty all the time: for having, for not having; for doing or not doing.

"What if...
We stopped celebrating busy as a measurement of importance?
What if instead, we celebrated how much time

we had spent listening, pondering, meditating, and enjoying time with the most important people in our lives?"

Greg McKeown

Happiness comes in many ways; at times it's so close we're scared to look at it. We can almost smell it and touch it. Yet rather than grab it, we run away. The reason? Our minds are set on survival mode and not on living mode, making things confusing and leading us to push enjoyment away. It's as if accepting happiness with open arms leads to joy disappearing. The warnings go off in our head:

- ✓ Is this addiction?
- ✓ Am I being lazy?
- ✓ Don't laugh, or you'll cry!
- ✓ A moment on the lips, a lifetime on the hips.

Does any of this ring a bell for you?

Embracing life and letting go

How many times have you felt you should be doing something else when you're relaxing and enjoying yourself? You feel guilty for sunbathing or watching a movie or having a dessert or cocktail. Instead, you think you should go to the gym, do housework or catch up on your emails, as if you have to fill every waking hour of your existence with doing, doing, doing.

It's as if we need to stop having fun and leave enjoyment for another time – a time that it is never right. When you allow this to happen, what are you telling your children (if you have them) or society? What are you saying yes to? What is the message?

Embrace life and live unapologetically, joyfully and happily – and without guilt about what you haven't done.

Let's face it, we're all going to die one day, and on that day things won't get done, and nobody will care how many belongings you amassed or how many certificates you put on the wall. You'll only take with you your experiences and the imprint of love on those you passed by in life; so make them worthwhile. How about living right now? It's a time for exploring all the fantastic opportunities available to you. When you find yourself putting off what you enjoy, ask: **"If I don't enjoy life now, when will I?"** Focus on what matters and start embracing life now.

That means bathing in life when it's good. If life calls for a lazy day, have a lazy day. Welcome it. Enjoy it! You do know best; trust your instincts and listen to your needs. Find the courage to say "NO" to society's rules. Show up in whatever way you want to by letting go. Even if it's a bad day, you can still give your very best, which might not be your best best, but hey! We are humans, not machines. Stay present in each moment by living it. Remember how important your life is to you and others and that you are worthy of all good things. Swap feeling guilty for celebrating your life.

Happiness, joy, and life do not last forever; embrace them while they last.

My grandma had glaucoma in her later days and eventually lost her sight completely. It still breaks my heart to remember her touching my new-born baby's face and hair so she could imagine what her great-granddaughter looked like. She told me once she would have done anything to get her eyesight back. It reminded me how easy it is to focus on things that don't matter. It's only when we lose something that we know what we had. My grandma wisely taught me to appreciate and celebrate life every day, not just special days.

The day I was writing this chapter, a finch flew right past my computer. I had a tiny bit of peach left on my plate and the little bird wanted it. Even though I was big and intimidating to it, the bird kept flying past me until it had the courage to land on my table and peck at the piece of peach. It took a chance and got what it wanted. You deserve to live life to the full, so be more like that bird. Give yourself a chance and allow your inner courage to emerge.

Empowering Actions

Write your answers to the following questions.

Step 1

Imagine yourself celebrating life, living in the moment then explore these questions:

- What does 'celebrating life' mean to you?
- How do you see yourself making the most of life?
- How do you feel when driven by balance and joy?
- What is the worst that can happen if you go all-in?
- What's the best that can happen if you embrace life?
- What impact will it have on your family if you're happy in your work and the way you interact with life?

Remember one decision can change your whole life forever. Best of all, it's you who makes that decision, so the power is in your hands. Life will be better than you expect when you start celebrating it.

Step 2

Write a list of everything that connects you to life – those things that make you feel on top of the world: positive, zesty and energised. When it's finished, put it somewhere you're likely to see it on a regular basis, e.g., on your phone screen, your fridge door, the bathroom mirror etc. Seeing this list helps you take action – and keeps you accountable. This is the list that will fire you up – like your vitamins for the day – supporting you to feel healthy, connected, grounded and happy.

Knowing what you enjoy is the first step to having a joyful life. Here are some ideas to get you thinking: knitting, martial arts, painting, swimming, golf, writing, family, friends, food, sex, music, boxing, meditation, walking in nature, reading, flowers, laughing, time alone, socialising, watching the sun set (or rise), a warm fire, dancing, driving, sailing, sport, fitness, pets, painting… the list is endless.

We all have different ways of embracing life, finding yours will give you a zesty approach to life.

Feeling zesty: a strong positive feeling that makes you feel alive. It ignites you and makes you feel inspired and a source of inspiration for others.

Remember that little bird? Well, for the entire week that I was writing outside, the little finch came to get a bit of peach or bread. He was braver every day allowing himself go a step further, until one day he took a whole slice of bread! Good on him, he trusted, risked and got what he wanted! He made me feel connected to life, and I celebrated his courage.

Zesty Takeaways

- ♥ There is no better time than now.
- ♥ Be courageous and celebrate every day!
- ♥ It's your right to be happy.
- ♥ Show up every day and say "yes", like a child.
- ♥ Explore what connects you with life.
- ♥ Life is better than we expect when we start celebrating it.
- ♥ **Embrace it while it lasts.**

Chapter 12

Touch and Joy

Touch is a rare commodity these days and when you arrive for your session, we talk about how, in a world of instant connection we are more disconnected than ever. Submerged in the world of technology and with the recent Covid-19 pandemic, people have stopped hugging and touching each other. And we acknowledge that not only do we miss it but how necessary it is. For most humans, touch is a source of Joy and we both agree that for us it is one of life's emotional essentials.

What happens when you don't moisturise your skin? It looks and feels dry, dull and lifeless, doesn't it? In the same way, when we don't experience the physical touch of another being, we become listless and unhappy.

The importance of physical touch

Love and touch play a primary role in the development of our psychological and physical wellbeing. They help us to connect with each other. Without them, we feel isolated and lonely among other things. Even though touch might seem like a luxury, it's a necessity for human health and wellbeing. It reduces cortisol and stress hormones and raises immunity.

Imagine having a dog and never petting it. You might give it a home and provide it with food, water and exercise but if you don't spend any time with it, the dog will get depressed. No love, no attention, no touch, no life other than its own, the dog will bark continuously, demanding attention because it's a pack animal and is hard-wired to feel a need to belong. It will literally go mad without play and companionship. Of course, humans are not dogs, this is just one example of the effect that affection has not only on dogs but on every living thing.

Hugs are free and we can never run out of them.

A few years ago, I went on holiday with my family to Lisbon in Portugal. One day, I was sitting on a bench checking my emails on my phone, I was so immersed in what I was doing that I'd become totally unaware of my surroundings. Suddenly, there was a pair of black eyes right in front of my nose. A woman was crouching down so she could get as close to me as possible. She was asking for money. She had saliva dripping from her mouth, she smelled unwashed and I could see that her clothes were dirty. All of which told me she was alone and living on the streets. I jumped up and told her she'd frightened me.

I dug a few coins out of my purse and gave them to her, hoping she would go away. I was worried she'd frighten my children. The woman recognised my accent and although we spoke different languages, we somehow struck up a conversation.

Then she looked into my eyes and asked me for a hug. I looked into her eyes and saw isolation, stress and despair. I hugged her but she held onto me. Then she asked me for another hug and for the second time, I could feel her pain, fear and loneliness run through my body. I held her tighter and a bit longer.

Soon after, holding my hand, she told me she was Brazilian. She told me how her mother and child had died, and how she didn't want to go on living because she no longer had anyone to love and be emotionally connected to.

She thought ending her life wouldn't be difficult when she lived in a world of solitude and drugs. Yet, in spite of what she said, she was there, hanging on to life. I sensed that she wanted to live.

This woman was scared. She felt unloved and desperate for affection and human touch. It was clear to me that she needed purpose in her life. She didn't want to die and there she was, like a nomad in a desert, looking for a drop of water, in need of human connection; I gave her what she asked for: hugs, warmth and a gentle smile. My encounter with this lady made me realise the necessity of physical touch for us as human beings. It's like moisture for our skin and water for our bodies, without it we're emotionally dry and dehydrated.

**Never underestimate the power of a hug,
it could save a life.**

Empowering Actions

Consider how important touch is by reflecting on these questions:

- How often do you hug your family and friends?
- Do you feel it is enough?
- If the answer is no, what benefit would you get if you did so more often?

How to get more physical contact in your life (when appropriate):

- Hug people as often as you can. Hugs are happiness on tap.
- Kiss your friends and family (if appropriate of course!), it'll make you feel warm inside. It is good for your brain, your hormones and your looks!

Hugs, kisses and smiles are important for our physiology. When you experience loving physical contact, your brain sends messages of thanks to your body. At the same time, the part of your brain that's in charge of emotions releases a lot of pleasure-inducing endorphins, serotonin and oxytocin; the hormones in charge of happiness. It's a win, win!

We don't know what love is yet, nobody knows. What we all know is how much we need it and, along with touch and other forms of connection, we are just beginning to realise how beneficial it is for our mental and physical wellbeing.

Touch and hug the people you love often and notice how you're able to handle stress far better.

Joy

Just as salt helps make our food taste better, joy makes our lives feel more vibrant. When we think of joy, our senses open up. Emotions are felt deeply, we see effortless beauty. Joy is like a soothing balm in our lives, making everything better, smoother and shinier.

Joy is essential for us emotionally and deciding to be joyful is a choice we can make daily.

We have all seen joy in a friend or loved one's face. Their expression changes instantly, radiating light and emanating grace. They look younger, with wrinkles appearing to smooth and eyes shining youthfully. Even their posture changes. Joy gives them a childlike attitude; they wear the world loosely and trust their surroundings.

What would life be like if we didn't invite joy into it? I say 'invite' because expressing joy is a choice we can make. It's a way of showing up in the world, no matter what. Now, more than ever as bad news is delivered with the speed of light, let's show up for each other with joy and renewed energy.

Joy is an emotion that loves to be shared. Unlike other emotions, joy loves freedom and likes to spread itself around.

Find your joy

- Make a list of everything that makes you feel joyful. When you think you've got everything down, go back and add more. There are always more ways to feel joyful than we think.
- Make a list of the most joyful moments in your life. The birth of a child, the signing of a contract, a special smile from someone you love. The day you published your book, met a special friend, baked a perfect cake or went sky diving. Whatever it is for you.
- As you read your list of joyful moments, choose the one you most enjoyed and relive it, remembering every detail. Imagine it as if it's happening again... Who's there? What's happening to make you feel so joyful? Where is it taking place? What are your surroundings? What can you hear, smell or taste? How do you feel? Experience all the emotions again.

Anchor your joy

Try this NLP technique, called anchoring, created by John Grinder and Richard Bandler. Anchors can be very useful in helping you access a resourceful state.

- Close your eyes and spend a few minutes immersing yourself in a joyful experience. Repeat it few times, making it sharper and clearer every time you remember it.
- As you get to the peak of your emotion touch your wrist to anchor this feeling, then break your state by opening your eyes.

- Repeat the experience several times so you anchor the state.
- The next time you want to conjure up those emotions again, touch your wrist to experience that wonderful feeling. Whenever you're sad or want to feel more joy, access this resourceful state by firing your anchor, reigniting that experience and reconnecting with it.

When you feel upset about something, despite all the obstacles, I invite you to find reasons to be joyful making it a daily choice. And when you do that, notice how alive you start to feel. It's easy to be upset, so I ask you to join me in spreading joy, leaving a legacy for the next generation.

"And perhaps
What made her beautiful
Was not her appearance
Or what she achieved,
But in her love
And in her courage,
And her audacity
To believe:
No matter
The darkness
Around her,
***Joy** ran wild in her,*
And that was the way
She came alive,
And it showed up in everything."

My adaptation of Morgan Harper Nicholls' poem

Zesty Takeaways

- Touching, kissing and smiling are some of life's emotional essentials.
- Possessions offer us comfort, touch offers us connection.
- Kiss it better, it'll help you cope in times of stress.
- Give and receive hugs as often as you can; they're happiness on tap.
- Joy is a choice you make, an attitude and a way to show up in the world.
- **Joy makes you happy, which says it all!**

Chapter 13

Let's Talk About Sex

When you visit, I usually make you a cup of tea or coffee. Today as I wait for the kettle to boil, I look at you and notice there's something different about you. So, without any further chat, I ask you how your sex life is.

You laugh a nervous though slightly cheeky laugh and pause to think about it. Maybe you need something stronger than tea to get you talking about sex!

Let's talk about sex

Sex is a natural and fun way of saying yes to life. It's also a subject that's uncomfortable for many people to talk about. Yet others see it as another way to celebrate life. There's still a lot of confusion about sex and how to approach it. When I was doing the research for this book, I talked to people about what they thought about sex, and most said they wanted to talk about it, even if it felt uncomfortable. In fact, I was asked to give it some attention in this book.

The general response was that most of us want to be able to talk about sex without feeling embarrassed. So, if you want to explore this subject, this is for you. After all, we deserve to not only have sex, but have good sex. And by that, I mean sex we have with consent, enjoyment and fun. Anything else isn't ever going to be good.

You think about what you eat and drink, also how much you sleep. You take care of your mental health and pay attention to what you're thinking. What about your sexual needs? Are you having good sex?

If you're not sure, the chances are that you don't know much about your sexual needs or what you're supposed to feel. Before you can have great sex, you need to know what you want – and why you might not be having as much of it as you'd like. Only then can you decide how to get more and better sex.

Apart from learning that people wanted me to talk about sex in this book, I also learned sex brings us many benefits, both emotionally and physically. For example, sex eases stress, improves sleep and lowers your blood pressure. It improves your immune system; helps you cope with pain and makes you look five to seven years younger!

Sex is another way of connecting to and embracing life, and another way of generating energy. It raises our body's vibration, adding a glow to our faces so we look as if we've slept for a week. When we have good sex, we're at ease with life. Sex is also great exercise and though you might not get a Jennifer Lopez bottom or a six-pack, you'll burn more calories than if you just sit on the sofa watching TV and eating ice cream!

Another advantage of sex is that it reduces the risk of a heart attack. And according to a study published in the American

Medical Association Journal, men who ejaculate at least 21 times a month are at less risk of prostate cancer. For women, sex helps to strengthen the pelvic floor muscles, which has a wide range of benefits as women age.

Yet there are challenges; having more and better sex – it isn't always as easy as it sounds. How, where and who you have it with depends on a variety of factors. And, like most things in life, the amount and quality of the sex you have is a conscious choice; it takes self-awareness and practice to have the sex of your dreams.

Empowering Actions

Think about your sex life for a minute, then answer these questions:

- What kind of sex life are you experiencing in your life right now?
- Is it the sex you want and dreamed of having?
- Are you sexually satisfied? If not, why not?
- How can you change this?

Next, imagine the sex life you would love to have… Allow your imagination to run wild, be brave and imagine the best sex life ever. Take some time to explore your fantasies for a while.

You can have this kind of sex life if you awaken your sexual desire and libido. We all have a sexual self – it's just waiting to be let out to play. We have to release it and give ourselves permission to enjoy it without shame or guilt. First, though, you need to find out how important sex is for you.

Sex? What sex?

The amount of sex we each have differs for many reasons, including our age, whether or not we have a partner, our lifestyle, work, family and health. All of these and much more can impact the amount of sex we're having. One client told me she'd heard so much about sex and how amazing it is that her expectations were sky high. When she had sex for the first time, it wasn't that good and she thought, "Is that it?" She felt really deflated and let down by her experience, to the point where she wasn't bothered about trying it again for quite some time. Maybe you can see her point?

My client and I spoke about how it was possible that she simply didn't have the right sexual partner or that neither of them really knew what they were doing or weren't in tune with their bodies. When I asked if she ever explored her own sexual responses, she told me she thought it was up her partner to know how to give her pleasure. She also told me that "girls don't do that", which is an old-fashioned perception that persists even though it's not true. And of course, men also have challenges, pressure and anxiety around sex. They worry about the size of their penis, their stamina and performance. There might be different reasons for anxiety around sex, it doesn't matter whether you're male or female, we all experience confusion about how to approach sex and our sexuality.

I have your attention now and as we sip our tea, you invite

me to tell you more. The first step is to understand your own physiology, sex organs and how they work. You can't expect your sexual partner to please you if you treat your own genitals as if they're a foreign part of you. So, explore your body to find out what you like and how you like it and change your beliefs and perceptions around sex.

Then communicate that to your partner and allow yourself to enjoy sex. You might not have done this before, and it doesn't matter. Relax, give yourself time and simply explore different sensations. At times, lack of awareness about our own body and what gives us pleasure is all that prevents us from having a good and healthy sex life.

Never leave your sexual satisfaction in the hands of someone else.

Don't have sex with someone who doesn't respect or value you. They won't offer you the sex you deserve, you'll be disappointed and your self-esteem will take a hit.

Communication is crucial

Is there a possibility that the reason your sex life isn't great is because you or your partner are stressed or haven't communicated what you each want? Or perhaps you simply feel too embarrassed to ask for what you want?

Communication with your partner is essential for enjoying sex. Things won't happen the way you want them to unless you talk to your partner and make sure you both understand what the other wants. If you don't, neither of you will know how to give pleasure to the other.

Knowing our boundaries is as important as understanding what we want sexually. It doesn't matter what or who it is, if it doesn't feel right, you need to let your partner know. Ask for what you want, otherwise you won't be able to change a mediocre sex life into an excellent and fun one.

Think about how your relationship would change if your sexual desires were satisfied and if you and your partner considered each other's desires?

The better the communication, the better the sex.

What's the worst that could happen when you ask for what you want? Take time to explore. If you don't get what you want, you'll find out where you stand, and what your partner feels about your request. And imagine you get what you want. Imagine that! How would it change the dynamics, bond and level of intimacy you have with your partner?

The quality of the sex you have is your responsibility, as is your sexual satisfaction.

Empowering Actions

- Play games and make sex fun. Remember, variety is the spice of life, so surprise your partner with something new and interesting to do together.
- Create an atmosphere to get you in the mood. If you're easily distracted by noise, play some music to block it out.
- Put a lock on your door, if you have children or make sure they're asleep. Take them to your parents or friends one afternoon so you have some intimate time. Come back home after the morning school run if you have the chance or simply find some time when in the shower.
- Switch off from the office, distractions or any other problems. It takes a lot of effort sometimes, but when you consider the benefits of making time for sex, it's worth it.
- Allow yourself space to transition from work-mode or the raised testosterone from exercise before starting to make love.

These simple practices help you ease the stress of the day and release energy so you can bring a sense of fun to your sex life.

If you find yourself putting off having sex, remember how good you feel afterwards and how much you love to share your intimate moments with your partner so you can build a stronger bond.

It's not so much about planning sex so it becomes robotic. It's about having it on your radar, so you don't forget about it. Live life intentionally even when thinking about sex.

Have sex on your terms, not anyone else's.

What gets in the way of sex?

The worst enemy of good sex is lack of time and energy: you're too tired, you don't have time, you have to care for small children, work is stressful… the list of distractions can be endless. Sadly, sex often falls to the bottom of our to-do lists. It seems that everything from everyday family life to hobbies and social media have priority over our sex life.

So, the one thing on your list that could probably stop you having a heart attack and sustain your wellbeing gets forgotten. How are you going to have great, life-affirming sex if you don't make time for it? You might believe your partner isn't interested in sex, but that might not be the case. It could be that they're bored or you've misunderstood their apparent lack of interest. For women in particular, there are other barriers to a great sex life, like a fear that they're not sexually attractive or that by asking for what they want they'll scare away their partner.

If you want something to change, you have to be the change you want to see in the world, and sex is part of that. If you want to be sexually healthy, you have to take the lid off the taboos that are getting in the way. So, take the lead and talk freely and naturally about it. Sex is fun and natural. It's not dirty or a sin or something you shouldn't discuss or that's only done to procreate. So, enjoy yourself. Why not? As I always say, if you don't do it now when you're healthy and able, when? Nothing lasts forever, not even our libido.

> *"Life is too short to not ask for what you want in a relationship, in bed, in your career or in your pizza."*
>
> Marie Forleo

Empowering Actions

- What would the sex of my dreams be like?
- Do I know what I like and dislike in bed?
- Do I love and accept my body?
- Am I honest with what is going on with myself and my partner?
- Do I make time for sex?
- Do I allow myself to enjoy sex?
- Do I have a healthy belief system around sex?
- Am I ready to ask for what I want? If not, what am I saying yes to instead?

Most of the time, if you think there's something wrong with your sex life, it's simply that you haven't given it enough attention or thought. Sometimes, things still don't work out, no matter how much you try. If that's the case, seek out professional help.

Zesty Takeaways

- Sex is beautiful and not a sin or something dirty. So, talk about it openly.
- The quality of the sex you have is your responsibility, so is your sexual satisfaction.
- Sex is another way of connecting to life and your partner.
- Better communication leads to better sex.
- **Never leave your sexual satisfaction in the hands of someone else.**
- Make it fun. Remember, variety is the spice of life.
- **Only have sex on your terms. If it doesn't feel good, say 'no'.**

Chapter 14

Your Inner Child

It's the beginning of the summer and the air is still warm, even though it's the end of the afternoon. The rush of the day is over and there is an explosion of colourful flowers everywhere. It's so inviting that we decide to sit outside in the garden. You sit on my old two-seater swing despite it being rusty and a bit worn. You notice this and mention it to me, but you don't seem to mind.

> *"Angels fly because they take themselves lightly."*
>
> G K Chesterton

I have put red polka dot bunting around the top of the swing to add some colour and it does the job. All this makes us both feel happy, connected and playful. We take off our shoes feeling like children again and it sets a relaxed tone for our session. We begin by talking about the child inside us, after all, as Woody Harrelson said, a grownup is a child with layers on.

The essence of you

It doesn't matter how old we are, we all have a child-like part deep within us. I like to call it our 'inner child' and it is the essence of who we are. It helps us connect and engage with life, which is good for our mental health and supports our creativity. That child within you is where the sparkle in your eye comes from; it's at the root of your ability to approach the world in a state of wonder.

Knowing and understanding ourselves more deeply adds another layer to living a life where we're true to who we are.

A healthy relationship with your inner child supports you in having fun and connecting you to the present moment. It is also another tool for developing bridges between the past and present so you can heal emotional pain. From the age of about seven or eight, we begin to separate from our innocent and happy inner child.

There are a number of reasons why this happens, from trauma and isolation to family loss, neglect or severe emotional or physical injury. Most of the time it's just part of growing up and preparing to go out into the world as an adult. We start to conform and follow the example of others around us. Before we know it, we begin to form beliefs about the world and how it should or shouldn't be. This process of maturing means we set aside the child within us and, just as we forget our childhood toys, so we stop connecting with our inner child and expressing our creativity.

Now and then our inner child screams at us because it wants to come out to play but is denied that freedom. We ignore its pleas, often for many years, blocking out the noise by focusing on our responsibilities and trying to conform.

Then one day we wake up feeling scared, lonely and even depressed. We feel and act small, the light has gone out of our eyes and our inner child has fallen silent. We wonder how this has happened and can't figure out why we've lost our enthusiasm for life.

And then we remember we have bullied ourselves into believing we had to be more, achieve more and have more. We think we've failed because we haven't got the job, house, children and partner we expected. We develop self-defeating behaviours and feel inadequate because we're not being the person somebody else wants us to be. We brainwash ourselves into believing we don't deserve love and respect. Eventually, we realise we've been giving all our attention to our inner critic rather than our inner child, and negativity has taken over our lives. Our inner child is hurt and that makes it challenging for us to regulate our emotions and manage our ability to make logical decisions.

Fortunately, there are many people who are in touch with their inner child, allowing this part of themselves to come to the surface. For them, there's lots of play and they celebrate who they are, keeping in touch with their essence. You can be one of them too and explore healthier ways of being.

Reuniting with your inner child is like rediscovering something you thought you'd lost a long time ago – and thought was gone forever. When you find it again, you appreciate it even more valuing its purpose in your life.

Of course, if your childhood was traumatic, you might not want to rediscover your inner child. If talking to that part of yourself is too difficult, you might want to consider talking to someone to help you understand, process and manage your emotions.

If you are willing to give it a go, smothering your inner child in love, compassion and understanding helps to heal the pain and so regulate your emotions, habits and responses. This could mean accepting past events and allowing yourself the opportunity to see them from a different perspective. Next, let's explore how you can connect your inner child to the physical world.

Empowering Actions

- Find a picture of yourself as a child, preferably at around six or seven years of age.
- Find a picture of yourself as you are now.
- Place the pictures beside each other and look at them together.
- As you look at the picture of yourself as a child, remember what you were like then. What did you like doing and what do you remember about your personality and attitude to life when you were happy.
- Breathe deeply and sit quietly until you feel centred and calm.
- As you reflect on this experience, ask yourself:
  - What would I gain from connecting with that part of me again?

- How did my inner child make me feel before I started to bury it?
- What have I lost by not connecting with that part of myself?
- What is the one thing I most want to say to my inner child?

Explore your inner child

The first time you do this exercise, make sure you're in a quiet place that's free from distractions. Practise it a few times and if it doesn't work the first time, don't be disappointed. Your deepest childhood feelings may bubble up, so when you begin to talk to your inner child again, you may find buried emotions coming to the surface.

Place your hand on your heart and explore the inner child in you by reaching out to a younger version of yourself – be prepared for surprises. If you haven't communicated with your inner child before, it might take some time before it makes its appearance. Be patient and gentle, you're accessing a different part of your subconscious, so it's important to ensure your inner child feels safe.

When your inner child surfaces, how is it feeling? Is it smiling? Does it look happy or upset? Does it seem scared or relaxed? Accept what you see and say sorry for your long absence.

Talk and listen to what your inner child has to say, even if you find it difficult to hear what it has to say. You might feel uncomfortable and that's okay; stay with it and explore whatever comes out.

Imagine giving your inner child a mental hug, love and the encouragement, comfort and time it needs and promise it that from now you're taking that part of yourself everywhere.

Return as often as possible to this exploration and repeat the steps until you notice, gently and slowly, that you're recovering the sparkle in your eyes and taking life lightly.

Care for your inner child

When you rediscover your inner child, you'll reframe your perspective on life making it easier to show up in the world as your true self. There's lots you can do to bring your inner essence back to life, like watching TV programmes that make you laugh, being silly, drawing or singing.

It's important to choose what you let into your life because you absorb energy from what's around you. If that energy is negative (like the news or someone who brings you down), it can take you to a bad place emotionally. If you spend your time watching soaps, the news or documentaries that fill you with guilt, fear and rage, it'll have a very negative effect on your mood. It'll impact the conversations you have, the way you look at the world and the way you approach your day.

Look for opportunities to raise your mood by reconnecting with your playful and creative inner child. Many of these are simple and easy to integrate into your day and can make a huge difference to how you feel.

Changing your habits can take time, so don't try to do everything at once. Allow yourself to be guided by what you enjoy. One of my clients rides her horse every week because it brings her peace and connects her with the childlike part of herself. My dad loves cartoons. They make him laugh out loud and forget about his worries for a while. Be compassionate and curious when exploring the playful part of yourself and if you ever feel ridiculous, remind yourself how much fun 'ridiculous' is and that the only ridiculous thing is to allow your essence to vanish.

Use your imagination

At the age of seven, Paola was diagnosed with idiopathic scoliosis in her back. When she was 18, she had a 10-hour operation to fix her spine. For the next four months, Paola had to stay completely still. Can you imagine being 18 and full of life but unable to move?

She told me how she mastered the art of relaxing and visualising. Every morning she would breathe slowly until she relaxed. Using visualisations, she would ask her inner child what she fancied doing that day. As a result, she went on many adventures using just her mind. She says she would not have been able to recover without the help and validation of her interior world.

Get active

Go for a walk or run, ideally in a park or anywhere in nature. If you can't do that, a walk in town can be beautiful too. Notice what's around you: how warm it is, how the sun and wind feel on your face, the colours you see and the people around you. Notice your breathing slowing down, soothing you. If you're walking to work, play some upbeat music to lift your energy and get you ready for the day ahead.

Things to do:

1. Sing out loud.
2. Smile at people for no reason.
3. Watch a movie you loved when you were a kid.
4. Make time to meditate.
5. Be creative: draw, paint, write, make music – whatever you enjoy.
6. Experience new things, something you always wanted to do and kept postponing.
7. Do some of the things you loved doing when you were young.
8. Write a list of your top five fun things to do – then *do* them.

Meditation

Meditation has countless benefits for your body as well as your mind and soul. It works best when you practise it regularly, even if it's only for a few minutes at a time. As you gain experience you can gradually build up to longer meditation sessions. Give it a go and see what happens; if you like it, make it into a habit.

- Sit in silence for a few minutes and breathe gently.
- As you relax, smile with your face then with your whole body.
- Keep breathing gently and smile with your entire being until you feel all the cells in your body beaming.

Stay with this experience for as long as you like and when you're ready, open your eyes.

As you learn how to focus for longer, you'll notice how your energy rises, making you feel calmer and more balanced.

Zesty Takeaways

- ♥ Stay in touch with your inner child, it's the essence of who you are.
- ♥ Explore what you love to do and what makes you smile.
- ♥ Your inner child loves to enjoy itself, so include lots of fun and creative activities in your life.
- ♥ Exploration and visualisation make your inner world richer, more relaxed and more creative.
- ♥ **Enjoy fun and being silly.**

Chapter 15

Gratitude

Today, you look radiant. You're excited about a new project you've started. You tell me how much lighter you feel and how you have more energy and confidence. We talk through what you've achieved in your personal and professional life since we began working together.

You tell me that you wish you'd thanked the teacher who'd taught you to be resourceful and to never give up as it's how you found me and came to work with me. I warm some bread and I lay it out on a board with cheese, cherry tomatoes and Spanish extra virgin olive oil, and we feel grateful.

Some say gratitude is an emotion, others a personality trait and I say it is both – and a choice as to how we show up in life. Two American psychologists, Emmons and McCullogh, conducted an experiment looking into the impact of gratitude on wellbeing. In their words, 'The results suggest that a conscious focus on blessings may have emotional and interpersonal benefits' and I very much agree. The benefits of practicing focused gratitude are countless. You can find out how to download their research in the Inspirations section of this book (see page 187).

"[Gratitude is] an emotion, an attitude, a moral virtue, a habit, a personality trait or a coping response."
Emmons and McCullough

A supersonic path to Happiness

Gratitude is the fastest way to happiness and wellbeing. Fortunately, it's easy to feel grateful when you are happy, so take the time to express gratitude and feel long-lasting happiness that doesn't vanish as soon as your situation changes; because gratitude, gives you the kind of happiness that isn't reliant on special moments. It raises your energy too and when you feel grateful, you feel lighter and have more energy. This is because the focus of your attention is on your appreciation for your surroundings and the people you're with. You pay attention to what you have rather than what you don't have and you count your blessings rather than cursing your misfortune. You become less judgemental, feeling happier and more content. Overall, you appreciate about what you previously took for granted.

You only need to feel ill for a day or two to appreciate your health and become aware that every second you're well and alive is an opportunity. Life really is a miracle, so let's appreciate it.

Gratitude is an attitude and a habit that can change your life. Sadly, some people never notice what they have because they're so focused on what's missing. They crave instant gratification, which never lasts. For them, nothing is ever enough. If you have people like this in your life, limit your time with them. Their judgemental attitude is a habit you definitely don't want in your life.

Empowering Actions

- Think of people around you who focus most of their attention on what they *don't* have, and drain your energy.
- Do these people seem satisfied with their life and do they show gratitude for what they have?
- These people might be members of your family or close friends, so you might feel conflicted and want to limit your time with them.
- Next, think about all the grateful people you know and think about how happy they are. How are they different from the other group of people?
- What sets them apart from others in your life?
- What do these people have in common?
- How does living in a state of gratitude impact their lives?

Aim to spend more time with these people as they will have a positive influence on you and will support you in living a life that's in line with your goals and ambitions. They're often great sources of support and inspiration.

How can you access gratitude?

By noticing what's good about life and noticing everything good that you have, from your eyelids to your material possessions is a practice I encourage you to build. It raises your energy and connects you to the source of life, something I learned about a long time ago and never fails to deliver.

When my two friends and I arrived in England in 1997, we didn't speak any English at all, which made it difficult for us to get jobs and find somewhere to live. One afternoon I went to a restaurant to ask for a job. There I met Pasquale, a Neapolitan chef. My first impression of him was that he was brusque and not very welcoming. He didn't offer me a job but he told me about his wife, who was also Spanish. A few days later, we met Teresa.

Make gratitude and appreciation a way of life.

Our friendship developed quickly, and we soon became a part of their family. Teresa and Pasquale were amazingly kind to us, inviting us to live with them while we found our feet. Even though they lived in a small flat and money was tight, they wouldn't take anything from us for rent, bills or food. We used their address so we could receive mail. We brought friends back at the weekend and we enjoyed lavish lunches and lovely family time with them. Their generosity was remarkable, and it taught us what kindness and gratitude really meant: giving and not expecting anything in return.

Pasquale and Teresa became like our second parents in the UK. Eventually, we learned English, got good jobs and were able to move out into our own place. But we never forgot what they did for us. We gave back with love and gratitude and visited them for the next 20 years until Pasquale died and Teresa returned to Spain. We all still visit Teresa whenever we can.

Empowering Actions

Show gratitude for the people who make your life easier and happier. Leave notes for them, saying how you feel. If you aren't great with words, draw pictures instead. Gratitude doesn't have to cost money. You could bake a cake or just spend quality time with them.

Share from your heart without expecting anything back.

On my morning walks, I get a flower or a sprig of lavender or rosemary to put it on my husband's breakfast plate as a sign of my appreciation. Words aren't needed; he knows what I want to say. I once met a guy who put a lollipop on his girlfriend's car windscreen every morning as a way of saying 'thank you, you mean a lot to me and I appreciate what you bring to my life'. Gratitude can be expressed in many ways, and you know the best way for the people who matter to you.

Empowering Actions

Gratitude journalling is a great way to enhance your wellbeing. It's a really easy way to rewire your brain, notice the good in your life and feel happier.

Begin by drawing a sun in your journal. Think of all the things, situations and people you are grateful for. Then write "I am grateful for..." in the sun's rays.

- On the first day of the week, write down five things you're grateful for.
- On the second day write 10 things you're grateful for.
- Keep increasing the number of things you're grateful for by five each day for the next five days until you're writing a list of 35 items each day. Even if it gets difficult – and it will – keep writing your gratitude list until you complete the task.

- After a week read what you have written. Keep your gratitude journal near to hand so you can re-read it often.

Make gratitude journaling a habit you practise every day, even if you only make the list in your head, rather than writing it down. You'll soon notice that you feel happier, more content and more aware of how amazing life is. Take a moment to appreciate how lucky you are to be here. As you begin to experience the benefits, you'll want to keep on doing it.

Appreciate unwanted gifts

One of my clients, Laura, had a hectic life. She had four children and they all went to different schools. Each did lots of after-school activities, including a lot of sports matches, which she attended. They also had an incredibly hectic social life.

One day, when she was driving her car, she fainted. The doctor said she would have her driving license taken away for a year for her safety and the safety of others. Soon after this happened, I started picking her up to take her to my house for our sessions.

She was telling me how inconvenient it was not to be able to drive and how it was turning her life upside down. I responded by suggesting that this bit of bad luck might be a gift rather than a curse, though she might not realise it right now. She wasn't very receptive to this idea and instead just felt even more irritated and frustrated by her situation.

For a while, life without her car was a huge inconvenience for Laura. And then one day, she told me, "I'm so grateful I can't drive at the moment. It's given me the time to reflect on my life and listen to what I want. When I could drive, I was always rushing around, so there wasn't any time to think, never mind just be. Not being able to drive has allowed me to take more care of my home and spend time with my friends. I've learned so much from being on my own too. I never had any time to myself before. It took a while to get used to it, and now I see the gift. I've reconnected with myself and found out what I really want. I'm grateful to everyone who's supported me during this time and I'm now grateful for what I have. I couldn't see it before."

As we sip our coffees, you share moments from your life when you felt the same. "Life has an uncanny way of revealing the treasure that's right under our noses." I say.

Then I ask you whether you remember the metaphor of the car I introduced you to at the start of our work together, and how gratitude helps us stay present so we can remain in the driving seat of our lives. You open your eyes wide. I can see you linking everything together in your mind. You lean back in your chair, breathing deeply and I know you're feeling grateful.

Place your hand on your heart and breathe deeply three or four times. Feel grateful for your heart pumping in your chest. Can you feel it? You are alive, very much alive and this is an opportunity to show your gratitude. **Gratitude is the secret weapon of a balanced and zesty life.**

"Gratitude gives me that funny feeling in my tummy
Like the sun about to burst.
It makes me happy; it makes me dance.
It makes me give; it makes me laugh.
Gratitude makes me feel jazzed."

Marina, Zest for Life

Zesty Takeaways

- Gratitude: the secret weapon for zesty living
- Your life is a miracle, appreciate it.
- Gratitude and ingratitude are both habits, so choose wisely!
- The benefits of gratitude include energy, happiness, radiance and connection.
- Don't expect to get anything back.
- If you're grateful to someone, let them know.
- **The supersonic way to happiness and wellbeing is gratitude.**

Chapter 16

Zest for Life Habits

When creating an extraordinary life, you can easily get out of balance because you put a lot of effort into one area of your life while neglecting others. Awareness is key here. Create your own stability in life with habits such as 'me time', creativity and fun. These support you in having a more rewarding, exciting and enjoyable life; making it easier to feel balance and live a life true to your authentic self.

Time for you

The best way to restore your energy is by spending time on your own. The morning is an especially good time for this. If you can, wake up earlier than anybody else in your house and start the day slowly. Enjoy the silence and space and disconnect from emails, your phone or any other tech for the first few minutes after you wake. Enjoy a warm drink and some soothing music. Do some meditation or simply allow yourself to have nothing else to do. Use this time to tune in and reset your energy and emotions. Express gratitude and appreciation for what you have. Remind yourself to be true to yourself and explore how you'd like your day to evolve, so you're focused, connected to your goals and in alignment. Make it a habit.

Respect yourself – If possible, avoid committing to too many meetings in one day. If you find yourself allowing draining events into your life, reflect on this. What are you saying yes to? Is this compromising your values? Make sure you are respecting yourself and your own needs by not conforming or seeking to please others. Keep rebalancing by staying aware of your behaviour so you can adjust whenever necessary.

Time – Give yourself room to breathe during your day by leaving some time to transition from one meeting, task or appointment to another. You'll be more effective and proactive if you do this.

Prioritise sleep – If you work long hours, expose yourself to pollution and deal with demanding people, make sure you get plenty of sleep. Taking work to bed isn't allowed!

Nourish your brain daily – Aim to learn something new by watching a documentary, listening to a podcast or reading a book. A great way to keep your mind fresh is to start a new hobby.

Make time to eat – It's important to nourish yourself with good food. If you feel tempted to miss a meal, remember that if *you* don't prioritise your needs, nobody else will. Of course, this isn't only about making time to eat, it's also about taking a break. When you give your brain a rest, you're more likely to come up with solutions to problems and have creative ideas.

Take care of your appearance – When you look your best, you feel your best. Maybe it's a case of applying a bit of lipstick, having a shave, getting a haircut or wearing clothes that make you feel good. Everything matters, and so do you.

Do work you love and get creative

We serve the world best when we do what we love. When you serve others by doing a job you don't like, it doesn't serve anybody, not you, not your company and not the world. It won't take long before you're worn out and resentful, making your life and the life of those around you unpleasant.

Find what you are good at then commit to it wholeheartedly. And if you don't know what that is, ask for help. Show up every day as if the world is depending on you. Be willing to make mistakes so you can learn faster. If you fall down, get up again and keep moving, no matter what challenges come your way.

Of course, doing what you love takes effort, commitment and passion, but it's worth it. It gives you the feeling of being in the right place at the right time, that your work is appreciated and what you do counts.

When at work, creating or networking, don't just talk to people so you can get something from them, like a sale or a useful contact. Aim to build lasting relationships with them by asking them how they are and making them feel noticed. Show them how important they are in your life and trust them because then they'll trust you. Be the difference that makes the difference by sharing your gifts with the world.

Time for fun

Whatever you do, have fun because nothing works if you don't enjoy it. Ask yourself whether you're happening to life or life is happening to you and reframe, actively creating your life and investing in making yourself happy. Prioritise your happiness and choose to have fun by setting time aside for it. You don't have to do anything expensive or time-consuming, it's about enjoyment.

Do some exercise, sing, dance, act, listen to music, read a book, take a bath, have a drink, talk to your loved ones or go out with friends – just do whatever makes you feel at your best.

Keep it simple and only include activities you value and enjoy.

Laughter is another choice you can make and a wonderful way to embrace life. It's also stimulating and good for your mental health. Adults and children laugh mainly when socialising, which is why the number of times you laugh depends on how much time you spend interacting with others. Studies show that children laugh an average of 300 to 400 times per day and adults only 17-18 times per day (see pages 187-189 for more on this).

Sebastian Gendry, founder of the online laughter university, says laughter connects and stimulates us. If we laugh often and for long enough, it can shift our physical and brain chemistry, drawing us out of our rigid thinking and shifting our energy from negative to positive, thereby changing our perception of life.

Laughter reduces stress hormones such as cortisol and adrenaline. It also improves your memory and lowers your blood pressure. That's not all, though. Amongst other things, it boosts your immune system and reduces the incidence and severity of depression. The benefits are countless, it ignites your zest for life and fires up your creativity.

Fun things to do

Play the 'how cool' game

Recently, a friend reminded me how she handled the prospect of returning to work after a holiday. This year, rather than moaning about going back to work, she decided to play the 'how cool' game. This deserves a little explanation... I was brought up in the 1980s when things that were exciting, new or good were described as 'cool'. The whole point of the game is to turn what might seem bad or unwanted into something good or exciting.

So, rather than saying, 'Oh no! I've got to go back to work tomorrow' and feeling miserable, she said, 'How cool, I have a job to go back to on Monday, I have a new year ahead of me that's full of possibilities. I get great holidays and great money to spend on enjoying myself by doing this job.

Life is simple, and so is this exercise. Don't complicate it or look for more. Simply add 'how cool' about anything you do that you want to change your feelings about. If the word 'cool' doesn't sit well with you, just use a different one instead

Using this simple phrase, you're going to feel lighter and those tasks you don't enjoy will feel less onerous. You'll smile more often and change your energetic vibration. At the very least, playing the 'how cool' game changes your awareness and gives you lots of food for thought and reasons to be grateful.

'How cool' examples:

- How cool, it is raining today, so I don't have to water the garden.
- How cool, the car won't start so I can take the tube rather than sitting in traffic.
- How cool, it's freezing outside and I have warm clothes and central heating.

Is it optimistic? Sure, it is. It doesn't matter how much it rains, the sun is always on the other side of the clouds. When you think about it, what other option is there? Does it take you to a better place? Yes. Life is what we make of it and sometimes all it takes is that change in perspective to remind us that for the most part, life is great.

Affirmations

How we talk to ourselves and others matters, as it reveals our view of ourselves and the world. Words are another way of expressing our beliefs. One powerful instrument in making that connection is affirmations.

When spoken intentionally, affirmations set the tone for the day and they filter through your brain making an impact on your life. Just parroting an affirmation won't have much of an impact. But if you set the intention with your heart, create a firm belief in what you're saying, and you're patient, you'll be surprised what happens. Affirmations are not magic, though they do help to shift behaviour. And when you change your behaviour, anything is possible.

Write down any affirmations that resonate with you on any particular morning and return to them throughout the day. Of course, the affirmations and support you might need on one day could be different to what you need on another. The best way to find the right affirmation for the day is to ask, 'What do I want to experience today that will support me in being the best version of myself for others?'

Look at the examples below and use them for guidance about how to create your own affirmations – or simply use them as they are written. Close your eyes, use your intuition and listen to what is relevant for you in your current situation.

Practise for a while and see what happens; after all, you've got nothing to lose and much to gain. My tip is that you only use a few affirmations at a time so you have clarity around where you're placing your attention. The first one on my list is my favourite, though I have been a bit naughty and included more than one affirmation in one sentence! It has become my belief and my reality.

- I am free and happy, I am healthy and sexy, and I live life with ease.
- Life supports me and loves me.
- I live a life of balance and congruence.
- I celebrate life.
- I live the full expression of myself.
- I accept change as part of my evolution.
- I do what I say I will do.
- I create glorious opportunities in my life and the lives of others.
- I am a creative human being.

- I create calm within myself.
- I am free to choose.
- I am caring of my body and kind to my mind.
- I am open to abundance in my life.
- I am the expression of who I love to be.
- I encounter life with love and joy.
- I am strong and I can handle everything that comes my way.
- I am vivacious and proactive.
- I believe in myself.
- I choose to change my experience at any time.
- I choose relationships that bring me joy.
- I give my personal best regardless of what I am doing.
- I am playful and in touch with my inner child.
- I am grateful for my life.
- I am true to my heart.
- I enjoy all the good that life has to offer.
- I trust my intuition.
- I empower myself and others around me.
- I like accepting and welcoming the new.
- I engage in authentic relationships.
- I listen to my body and mind when they are tired.
- I have fun with what is available to me.
- I laugh with no agenda.
- Even though life is far from perfect, it's still great.

Practise and you'll soon find you can handle whatever comes your way. Ah, we have so many incredible resources at hand, and of course music is good for the soul. I firmly believe life is better with music!

Music for the soul

I went to a club with some friends in Brighton and magic was happening. People from all walks of life, social backgrounds and cultures were united under one roof enjoying the same thing: music. No one cared what you did for a living or who you were. The ambience was electrifying. We all understood each other because we were connected by music. Music was an energy that made us feel alive.

"I think of music in itself as healing.
It's an explosive expression of humanity.
It's something we are all touched by,
no matter what culture we're from."

Billy Joel

Eight benefits of music

1. Music raises your mood. You can probably remember many times when you've used music to make yourself feel better.

2. Music makes you feel safe. When you were a child, did you ever sing when you were frightened? Playing music can take your mind off whatever is scaring you and makes you feel comforted and safe.

3. Music diminishes pain. I remember when I was stung by a wasp and singing was the only way I could cope with the pain.

4. Music calms anger. Some people sing when they are angry, it helps them snap out of their negative mood.

5. Music helps you focus. Many people listen to music when they want to concentrate because it helps to block out distractions.

6. Music can be used to set your energy for the day. I deliberately play the same song by Coldplay, Amazing Day, every morning. I find it soothing, it puts me in a great mood and raises my energy. Choose your own version of Amazing Day and play it daily.

7. Music stimulates your memory. Have you ever heard a song and found yourself instantly taken back to a specific time and place? Do it now; think of a song that brings you awesome memories.

8. Music has a powerful effect on memory and it's being used more and more to help patients with dementia and Alzheimer's to reconnect with life. I recently found a YouTube video about a study conducted at a nursing home for those with Alzheimer's. These patients were in a state of inertia. Despite many stimuli around them, they'd stopped engaging with others. And they came alive when they listened to the music of their youth. The following story stood out for me. It's called 'Henry Wakes Up!'

> *Henry has been unresponsive for more than 10 years and is almost un-alive in a nursing home (as his doctor describes it). Then one day, he's given an iPod loaded with his favourite music. As he listens, he lights up. His eyes move, his body rocks and his mouth sings.*
>
> *After listening to the music, Henry can hold a lucid conversation. It's amazing to watch. As his doctor says, "Somehow Henry has been restored to himself, he has remembered who he is, and he has reacquired his identity through the power of music."*
>
> *Henry himself explains how the music has allowed him to feel love again, "I feel a bundle of love and dreams. It gives me a feeling of LOVE."*

Magical stuff.

Here are some other benefits of music that have been discovered by scientists.

- Music makes you happier.
- Music enhances the performance of runners.
- Music lowers stress and improves health.
- Music helps you sleep better.
- Music reduces depression.
- Music helps you eat less.
- Music elevates your mood while driving, so you stay more alert.
- Music strengthens your capacity for learning and enhances your memory.

- Music relaxes patients before and after surgery.
- Music reduces pain.
- Music helps Alzheimer's patients remember who they are.
- Music improves recovery in stroke patients.
- Music increases verbal intelligence.
- Music raises IQ and academic performance.
- Music keeps your brain healthy in old age.

Don't take my word for it, just close your eyes, listen to some music and see what emotions come up for you.

There are no corners that music can't reach or emotional places it cannot heal. There is music to suit all moods, cultures and tastes. If I was a doctor, I'd give you a prescription for a dose of music. Music is a positive influence on most people's life and when I interviewed friends and clients for this chapter, one person said, "life without music feels like a broken instrument: dead." Another person told me: "Life without music is a long and dark tunnel; life with music on the other hand, it is like the soundtrack of a film, reflecting the emotions of the day and bringing back memories. Life and music are synonyms."

"Music and rhythm find their way
into the secret places of the soul."

Plato

Zesty Takeaways

- ♥ Music connects you with yourself and life.
- ♥ Music brings people together.
- ♥ Music can heal, calm and relax us, helping us feel happy, motivated and energised.
- ♥ Music stimulates your memory.
- ♥ **Music finds the way into the secret places of your soul.**

Does it sometimes feel as if 'the grass is always greener on the other side'? Well, maybe it is or maybe it isn't. All you need to do is take care of the grass on *your* side! Now go and water your life and watch your grass grow. You know what to do!

Where Do You Go From Here?

Your presence fills my kitchen. We are discussing how being in the driving seat of your life and fully awake has led you to change your habits and the way you respond to life. Changing what was happening on the inside has changed what's happening in your life. You now trust your ability to handle life using the many resources you have available to you. Thank you for exploring the best you and for coming back to your true self. Your whole persona projects balance and congruence. Now go and share your gifts with the world and start making of your life whatever you want it to be.

You are self-aware, awakened and in charge of your life. Even more, you've gone from limiting to limitless. Yes, it takes an inner revolution to find inner freedom and balance, and it was worth it. Your life and its results depend on you as it does not matter what the situation is, you can always turn the wheel in a different direction.

Live a life of endless possibilities

You have a life of endless possibilities ahead of you. Go wherever you want to go from here. Whatever journey you choose, create a checklist to make sure everything goes as you want it to.

What is your attitude? Just as fourteen hours of the same music can be boring, so it can be dull to approach everything with the same attitude. So, make sure you have a selection of approaches to keep it lively.

Choose with care who you travel your life with. Bring along the people you love and who stimulate you, those who bring out the best in you and make you want to sing. If you get lost and can't see the way ahead, *trust your inner-built in navigation system,* it always knows best.

Take responsibility for your safety and the safety of those travelling with you by stopping to take a rest along the way so you can look after yourself.

You have awareness and clarity as to what you want; at the very least be ready to have fun and live with a clear intention.

Make of your life your passion, adding love, fun, and gratitude.

Put your vision into action and when you get results, play like a child and celebrate. Scream, laugh, pray that you'll never stop playing, and dance. Share it with others. Not everybody gets this chance!

You are a human being, so act like one, feel like one, love like one; and whatever you have in mind, start now, now, now. If you wait to be ready, you'll miss life.

You have all that you need, so go outside and play big, let your zest for life be contagious; spread it around you like summer heat.

You have become excellent at living a life that it is true to yourself, and you're living a balanced, zesty life. By doing this you influence and inspire others in this world. And this can be your legacy, leaving this planet better than you found it.

In an ever-evolving world,
Live and Love,
Marina, Zest for Life

"Never doubt that a small group of thoughtful, committed citizens can change the world; indeed, it's the only thing that ever has."
Margaret Mead

Inspirations

Books

Banks, Sydney, 'The Three Principles', https://threeprinciplesfoundation.org/

Burchard, Brendon, *High Performance Habits*, Hay House, 2017

Cope, Andy; Oattes, Gavin and Hussey, Will: *Zest*, 2019, Capstone

Knight, Sue, *NLP At Work: The difference that makes the difference*, Nicholas Brealey Publishing; Revised edition (2020)

Madden, Florence and Sarantinou, Eleni: *Everyday NLP: For life, work and relationships*, Everyday NLP, 2019

Other references

"Shoulda, woulda, coulda, are the last words of a fool"
Lyrics by Beverly Knight and Craig Wiseman

Emmons & McCullough, 'Counting blessings versus burdens: An experimental investigation of gratitude and subjective well-being in daily life', *Journal of Personality and Social Psychology*, 2003, Vol 84, No. 2, pp 377-389

Sex Prevents Prostate Cancer
Sarah Hiner president of Bottom Line Inc (https://www.bottomlineinc.com), interviews Dr Geo Espinosa ND https://youtu.be/-ebarqQIAisS

Suzana Herculano-Houzel
http://www.suzanaherculanohouzel.com/

'What Happens Inside Your Brain When You Listen to Music, in Three Mind-Blowing GIFs' https://www.mic.com/articles/119856/this-is-what-happens-inside-your-brain-when-you-hear-a-song

Henry wakes up! https://youtu.be/Fw7Y78aqf_I

Martin Kuiper NA, *Daily occurrence of laughter: Relationships with age gender and Type A personality.* International Journal of Humor Research, 12(4), 355-384

Radical remission from cancer: RadicalRemission.com

Inspiring Reads

All references are to paperback editions

Brown, Jeff, *Spiritual Graffiti*, Enrealment Press, 2015

Brown, Brené: *The Gifts of Imperfection*, Hazeldon Publishing, 2010; *Daring Greatly*, Penguin Life, 2015; *Rising Strong*, Vermilion, 2015

Dispenza, Dr Joe, *Becoming Supernatural: How Common People are Doing the Uncommon,* Hay House, 2017

Doyle, Glennon, *Untamed: Stop Pleasing, Start Living,* Vermillion, 2020

Forleo, Marie: *Everything is Figureoutable*, Penguin, 2020

Gilbert, Elisabeth, *Eat, Pray, Love,* Bloomsbury, 2007

Hay, Louise: *You Can Heal Your Life,* Hay House, 1984

Jeffers, Susan, *Feel the Fear And Do It Anyway: How to Turn Your Fear and Indecision into Confidence and Action,* Vermillion, 2007 (revised edition)

Jeffers, Susan, *Embracing Uncertainty: Achieving Peace of Mind as we Face the Unknown,* Hodder Paperbacks, 2003

Kline, Nancy, *Time to Think: Listening to Ignite the Human Mind*, Cassell, 1999

Pinkola Estés, Clarissa, *Women Who Run with the Wolves: Contacting the Power of the Wild Woman*, Rider, 2008

Ruiz, Don Miguel and Mills, Janet, *The Four Agreements: A Practical Guide to Personal Freedom*, Amber-Allen Publishing, 2011

Tolle, Eckart: *The Power of Now: A Guide to Spiritual Enlightenment*, Yellow Kite, 2001

Video

Watch Marie Forleo's award-winning show MARIETV https://marieforeleo.com

Dr Wayne Dyer: watch all his videos https://drwaynedyer.com

Meditation

If you'd like more guidance and resources for meditation practice check out https://mindfulyou.space.

About the Author

Marina Fernández Julián, born and raised in Granada, Spain, It was her curiosity for life that took her to Brighton in the UK, where she has lived for more than 20 years with her husband and two children.

Described by many as vibrant, vivacious and full of life, Marina's passions are sharing home, food and laughter with family and friends. A coach and NLP trainer she knew from an early age her purpose in life was to support others to thrive.

Her work has centred on transforming limited thinking into freedom of thought, helping clients to climb to self-awareness and the next level of consciousness enabling them to live a life driven by them. **A life true to themselves.**

To sum it up in one sentence, she supports others to reclaim their stories, inner freedom and joy in life. This results in proud, confident and powerful individuals who are experts at being themselves and living a life of excellence.

Marina works with adults and teenagers, and believes this self-evolving journey is for anyone and everyone to start at any time of their lives. Her book comes at a poignant time when we have been living through uncertain times without our usual connections.

Marina's work helps to empower people, which in turn allows their friends, family and other connections to live with more harmony and balance too. Each one of these connections give permission to another to live their own self-driven lives and so create a more balanced connected world.

The aim of this book is to enable YOU to live a life that is balanced and true to yourself, fully in charge of your story, so you can live your dreams, thrive and love the life you choose.

Get the FREE Guide *The 11 Pillars of Inner Balance* at https://www.marinazestforlife.com/balance-giveaway

Work with Marina

If you'd like to thrive further and want to continue this conversation, work with Marina on your self-development journey with real time bespoke sessions to suit your needs. Email and subscribe to her website for free tools. Whether you are an individual looking for personal coaching or want in-company training solutions, she will be there for you.

In addition to one-to-one coaching she delivers training for teenagers on a one-to-one basis and in schools as she knows these young people are the leaders of the future. Her passion is to support teenagers who are driven and enthusiastic about life knowing who they are. If you are a parent wanting to give your child a head start check **The Giant Child Program – Learning for the leaders of the future**.

Contact:

Email: Marinazestforlife@gmail.com
For free tools and inspiration check and subscribe at
https://www.marinazestforlife.com
Instagram: @marinazestforlife
Facebook: Marina ZEST for LIFE
LinkedIn: Marina Fernández Julián

Thank you for taking the time to read my book. I would love to hear what you think of it and if you could leave a review on Amazon, that would be fantastic.

Many thanks
Marina, Zest for Life